Profiles of Supremely Creative People

Shah Rukh

Published by Shah Rukh, 2024.

PROFILES OF SUPREMELY CREATIVE PEOPLE

First edition. June 30, 2024.

Written by Shah Rukh.

Table of Contents

Prologue

In a world driven by the ordinary, it is the extraordinary that illuminates our paths. Creativity, that elusive force, shapes our reality and transcends the boundaries of time, culture, and discipline. It is a spark that ignites revolutions, a whisper that inspires masterpieces, and a vision that redefines the limits of human potential. This book, *Profiles of Supremely Creative People*, is a tribute to those who have harnessed this force to leave indelible marks on history.

From the Renaissance genius of Leonardo da Vinci to the futuristic visions of Elon Musk, the journey of creativity is as diverse as it is profound. These individuals, with their relentless curiosity and unyielding dedication, have dared to dream differently, think unconventionally, and create fearlessly. They have painted on the canvases of art, science, literature, music, and technology with colors that defy convention and challenge the status quo.

Creativity is not a gift bestowed upon a select few; it is a universal potential that resides within each of us. Yet, what sets these luminaries apart is their ability to transform their visions into reality, often against insurmountable odds. Their stories are not just tales of brilliance but also of resilience, perseverance, and the courage to embrace failure as a stepping stone to success.

In the chapters that follow, we will delve into the lives of remarkable individuals. Each chapter is a window into their worlds, offering glimpses of their struggles, triumphs, and the creative processes that fueled their extraordinary contributions. From the introspective solitude of Vincent van Gogh to the innovative laboratories of Marie Curie, we will explore the myriad ways in which creativity manifests and evolves.

This book is not merely a compilation of biographies; it is an exploration of the essence of creativity itself. It seeks to inspire, to provoke thought, and to celebrate the boundless potential of the human spirit. As we traverse the landscapes of their minds, let us remember that their stories are not just their own. They are reflections of our collective ability to dream, create, and transform the world.

Welcome to the journey of discovering the alchemy of creativity. Welcome to *Profiles of Supremely Creative People*.

Chapter 1: Leonardo da Vinci

Leonardo da Vinci, often hailed as the quintessential "Renaissance man," embodies the pinnacle of human creativity and intellectual prowess. Born on April 15, 1452, in Vinci, Italy, he was an illegitimate son, a fact that would influence the unique path of his education and his life. From a young age, Leonardo displayed a prodigious talent for art, and he was apprenticed to the renowned artist Andrea del Verrocchio in Florence. This apprenticeship was not merely a period of learning techniques; it was a time of immersion in a milieu of artistic and scientific inquiry that profoundly shaped Leonardo's approach to creativity and knowledge.

Leonardo's artistic achievements alone would cement his place in history. His works, including the enigmatic "Mona Lisa" and the monumental "Last Supper," are masterpieces that demonstrate an unparalleled mastery of technique, composition, and emotion. The "Mona Lisa," with her mysterious smile and captivating gaze, remains one of the most iconic and studied paintings in the world. Its subtle use of sfumato, a technique of blending colors and tones to achieve a soft, realistic effect, showcases Leonardo's innovative approach to painting. "The Last Supper," depicting the moment Jesus announces one of his disciples will betray him, is a triumph of perspective and human emotion, capturing the varied reactions of the disciples in a way that had never been done before.

But to reduce Leonardo to just a painter would be a gross understatement. He was a polymath whose interests spanned an extraordinary range of disciplines, including anatomy, engineering, botany, geology, and mechanics. His notebooks, filled with detailed sketches and observations, reveal a mind constantly inquiring and experimenting. These notebooks, which cover topics as diverse as the anatomy of the human body and the mechanics of flight, provide a window into his relentless curiosity and his method of learning through observation and experimentation. One of his most famous sketches, the "Vitruvian Man," is a study of the proportions of the human body and represents the fusion of art and science that was at the heart of Leonardo's genius.

Leonardo's fascination with the human body led him to conduct dissections and produce some of the most accurate anatomical drawings of his time. His studies in anatomy were not just for the sake of science; they informed his art, allowing him to portray the human form with unprecedented accuracy and vitality. These anatomical drawings were so advanced that they would not be surpassed for centuries. His sketches of muscles, bones, and organs are not only scientifically valuable but also artistically stunning, showcasing his ability to see beauty in the complexity of the human form.

In the realm of engineering, Leonardo's imagination was boundless. He conceived designs for machines that were centuries ahead of their time, including early concepts of helicopters, tanks, and submarines. While many of these designs were not realized in his lifetime, they demonstrate his visionary thinking and his ability to merge art and engineering in ways that continue to inspire. His studies of water flow, mechanical devices, and fortification systems reveal a deep understanding of physics and mechanics, and his designs for bridges, catapults, and flying machines showcase his ability to think in three dimensions and anticipate modern engineering principles.

Leonardo's interest in nature was profound, and his botanical studies reflect his meticulous observation of plants and their structures. He approached the study of plants with the same rigorous eye for detail that he applied to his anatomical studies, producing drawings that are both scientifically accurate and artistically beautiful. His observations on the growth patterns of plants, the way they responded to light, and their internal structures contribute significantly to the field of botany. These studies also informed his art, as seen in the detailed and realistic depictions of plants and flowers in his paintings.

One of the most remarkable aspects of Leonardo's genius was his ability to connect seemingly disparate fields of knowledge. He understood that the principles governing the mechanics of the human body could be applied to machines, that the way light interacted with objects could enhance his paintings, and that the patterns found in nature could inform his designs. This integrative approach to knowledge is a hallmark of his creativity, allowing him to innovate in ways that few others could.

Despite his incredible talents and achievements, Leonardo's life was not without struggles. His notebooks reveal a man often frustrated by his own perceived shortcomings and the limitations of his time. He was known for his habit of starting numerous projects, many of which were left unfinished. This tendency has been attributed to his insatiable curiosity and his desire to explore new ideas continually, rather than a lack of discipline or commitment. His work was also constrained by the political and social upheavals of his time, including wars and the shifting fortunes of his patrons.

Leonardo's legacy is immense and multifaceted. His art continues to be celebrated for its beauty and technical mastery, while his scientific studies and inventions demonstrate a profound understanding of the natural world and the principles that govern it. His notebooks, filled with drawings, diagrams, and musings, remain a testament to his boundless curiosity and his unique ability to see the interconnectedness of all things. They offer insights into the mind of a genius who was constantly questioning, exploring, and pushing the boundaries of what was known.

In the broader context of the Renaissance, Leonardo represents the ideal of the well-rounded, intellectually curious individual who seeks to understand and contribute to many fields of knowledge. His work embodies the spirit of inquiry and innovation that defined the period, and his influence extends far beyond his own time. He is a figure who bridges the gap between art and science, showing that creativity and analytical thinking are not mutually exclusive but can enhance and enrich one another.

Leonardo da Vinci's life and work continue to inspire and captivate people around the world. His ability to blend art with science, to find beauty in the natural world, and to imagine possibilities far ahead of his time, makes him a timeless symbol of human potential. His legacy is a reminder that creativity knows no bounds and that the pursuit of knowledge and beauty is a noble and enduring endeavor.

Chapter 2: Michelangelo Buonarroti

Michelangelo Buonarroti, born on March 6, 1475, in Caprese, Italy, stands as one of the most influential and multifaceted artists in Western history. A master of the Renaissance, he excelled in painting, sculpture, architecture, and poetry, leaving an indelible mark on each field. His prodigious talent was evident from a young age, and he was recognized as a genius by his contemporaries, who referred to him as "Il Divino" (The Divine One). Michelangelo's work is characterized by an unparalleled understanding of the human form, an intense emotional depth, and a powerful expression of divine beauty.

Michelangelo's artistic journey began in Florence, a city that was the heart of the Renaissance and home to some of the greatest artists and thinkers of the time. At the age of thirteen, he was apprenticed to the painter Domenico Ghirlandaio, who was impressed by his talent and quickly saw his potential. During his apprenticeship, Michelangelo gained a solid foundation in the techniques of fresco painting, which would later serve him well in his monumental works on the Sistine Chapel ceiling. However, Michelangelo's true passion lay in sculpture, and he soon began to study under the sculptor Bertoldo di Giovanni, who introduced him to the works of classical antiquity and the principles of human anatomy.

Michelangelo's early works, such as the "Battle of the Centaurs" and the "Madonna of the Steps," already demonstrate his keen interest in the human form and his ability to infuse his figures with a sense of movement and emotion. These works also reflect his deep admiration for the art of ancient Greece and Rome, which he studied avidly. His early exposure to classical sculpture profoundly influenced his artistic style, leading him to create works that combined idealized beauty with a striking realism.

One of Michelangelo's most famous sculptures, the "Pietà," created between 1498 and 1499, is a masterpiece of Renaissance art.

Commissioned for the French cardinal Jean de Bilhères, the "Pietà" depicts the Virgin Mary holding the dead body of Christ in her lap. The sculpture is remarkable for its emotional intensity, exquisite detail, and the serene beauty of Mary's face, which contrasts with the tragic subject matter. Michelangelo's ability to convey the sorrow and resignation of Mary, while maintaining an idealized and almost ethereal beauty, showcases his extraordinary talent for capturing human emotion in marble.

In 1501, Michelangelo returned to Florence, where he was commissioned to create a statue of David. The resulting work, completed in 1504, is one of the most iconic sculptures in art history. Standing over 17 feet tall, Michelangelo's "David" represents the biblical hero at the moment before his battle with Goliath, embodying both physical perfection and inner resolve. The statue's dynamic pose, meticulous anatomical detail, and intense expression make it a powerful symbol of the human spirit's triumph over adversity. "David" also reflects Michelangelo's deep understanding of human anatomy and his ability to infuse marble with a sense of life and movement.

In addition to his prowess as a sculptor, Michelangelo was a masterful painter. His most celebrated painting project is undoubtedly the Sistine Chapel ceiling, which he completed between 1508 and 1512. This monumental work, which spans over 5,000 square feet, contains some of the most famous frescoes in the world, including the "Creation of Adam," the "Last Judgment," and the "Creation of Eve." Michelangelo's ability to organize such a vast composition and his use of vibrant colors, dramatic lighting, and complex poses demonstrate his extraordinary artistic vision and technical skill. The Sistine Chapel ceiling is not only a masterpiece of Renaissance art but also a profound expression of theological and philosophical ideas, depicting the story of humanity's creation, fall, and redemption.

The "Creation of Adam," perhaps the most iconic image from the Sistine Chapel, illustrates the moment when God gives life to Adam.

The nearly touching hands of God and Adam have become a symbol of divine creation and the connection between the human and the divine. The composition's dynamic energy, the detailed rendering of the human body, and the expressive faces of the figures reflect Michelangelo's deep understanding of both human anatomy and the power of visual storytelling.

Michelangelo's work on the Sistine Chapel did not end with the ceiling. Between 1536 and 1541, he returned to paint "The Last Judgment" on the altar wall. This immense fresco depicts the second coming of Christ and the final judgment of souls, with a dramatic array of figures representing the blessed and the damned. "The Last Judgment" is notable for its complex composition, emotional intensity, and the dynamic poses of its figures, which reflect Michelangelo's evolving style and his preoccupation with themes of salvation and divine justice.

Beyond painting and sculpture, Michelangelo also made significant contributions to architecture. In 1546, he was appointed chief architect of St. Peter's Basilica in Vatican City, one of the most important architectural projects of the Renaissance. Michelangelo's design for the basilica's dome, which was completed after his death, remains one of the most recognizable and influential structures in the world. His work on the basilica showcases his ability to integrate architecture with sculpture and his understanding of space and form, creating a building that is both a functional place of worship and a monumental work of art.

Michelangelo's architectural achievements also include the design of the Laurentian Library in Florence, which demonstrates his innovative approach to space and his mastery of both classical and contemporary architectural elements. The library's dramatic staircase, with its flowing curves and dynamic forms, reflects Michelangelo's ability to infuse architecture with a sense of movement and energy, transforming a utilitarian space into a work of art.

In addition to his artistic achievements, Michelangelo was a prolific poet, writing over 300 sonnets and madrigals. His poetry reflects his deep philosophical and religious beliefs, his struggles with artistic creation, and his reflections on love, beauty, and mortality. Michelangelo's poems, often intensely personal and introspective, provide insight into his inner life and his views on the nature of art and the role of the artist. His literary work, like his visual art, reveals a mind deeply engaged with the fundamental questions of human existence and the search for meaning and beauty.

Michelangelo's life and work were not without challenges and controversies. He had a complex relationship with his patrons, including the powerful Medici family and several popes, who often made demands that conflicted with his artistic vision. Despite these conflicts, Michelangelo maintained a fierce independence and a dedication to his artistic principles, often working tirelessly to complete projects that would stand the test of time. His intense work ethic, combined with his extraordinary talent, allowed him to create some of the most enduring works of art in history.

Michelangelo's influence on Western art is profound and far-reaching. His innovative approach to the human figure, his ability to convey complex emotions through his work, and his integration of art and architecture set new standards for artistic excellence. His works have inspired countless artists, from his contemporaries in the Renaissance to modern-day sculptors and painters, who continue to draw on his techniques and his vision.

The legacy of Michelangelo is not limited to his artistic achievements; he also represents the Renaissance ideal of the "universal man," an individual who excels in multiple disciplines and seeks to understand and express the complexities of the human condition. His life and work exemplify the spirit of curiosity, creativity, and intellectual rigor that defined the Renaissance and continue to inspire people around the world.

Michelangelo Buonarroti's contributions to art, architecture, and literature make him a towering figure in the history of Western culture. His ability to transform marble into lifelike figures, his mastery of the fresco technique, his innovative architectural designs, and his deeply personal poetry all reflect a unique and profound artistic vision. His work not only captures the beauty and complexity of the human experience but also explores the relationship between humanity and the divine, offering insights that remain relevant and inspiring today. As one of the greatest artists of all time, Michelangelo's legacy endures, reminding us of the power of creativity and the enduring quest for beauty and meaning in our lives.

Chapter 3: William Shakespeare

William Shakespeare, often referred to as the Bard of Avon, is arguably the most influential writer in the English language and a towering figure in world literature. Born on April 23, 1564, in Stratford-upon-Avon, England, Shakespeare's works have transcended time and cultural boundaries, continuing to captivate audiences and readers more than four centuries after his death in 1616. His plays, sonnets, and poems explore the breadth of human experience, delving into themes of love, power, jealousy, betrayal, ambition, and the supernatural with unparalleled insight and eloquence.

Shakespeare's life began in the modest market town of Stratford-upon-Avon, where he was born to John Shakespeare, a successful glover and alderman, and Mary Arden, the daughter of a wealthy landowner. He was the third of eight children and received a basic education at the local grammar school, where he likely studied Latin, classical literature, and rhetoric. This foundation in the classics would later influence his writing, as he drew upon a wide range of sources for inspiration, including Roman and Greek mythology, historical texts, and contemporary works.

At the age of 18, Shakespeare married Anne Hathaway, who was eight years his senior. The couple had three children: Susanna and the twins Hamnet and Judith. Little is known about Shakespeare's early adulthood, but it is believed that he moved to London in the late 1580s or early 1590s, where he began his career as an actor and playwright. By 1592, he had established himself in the London theater scene, as evidenced by a disparaging reference to him by the playwright Robert Greene, who accused him of being an "upstart crow" who dared to compete with more established writers.

Shakespeare's early plays, such as "Henry VI" and "Titus Andronicus," reflect the influence of his predecessors, including Christopher Marlowe and Thomas Kyd, and demonstrate his burgeoning talent for dramatic storytelling and complex character development. These early works, while not as polished as his later masterpieces, showcase his ability to craft compelling narratives and his keen interest in historical and political themes.

The 1590s were a period of remarkable productivity and artistic growth for Shakespeare. During this decade, he wrote a series of history plays, including "Richard III," "Henry IV," and "Henry V," which explore the complexities of political power, the responsibilities of leadership, and the impact of war on both rulers and their subjects. These plays are notable for their rich characterizations, intricate plots, and the way they blend historical events with dramatic fiction, providing a nuanced and often critical perspective on the nature of kingship and governance.

In addition to his history plays, Shakespeare penned some of his most beloved comedies during this period, including "A Midsummer Night's Dream," "Much Ado About Nothing," "As You Like It," and "Twelfth Night." These comedies are characterized by their wit, humor, and exploration of themes such as love, identity, and social conventions. Shakespeare's comedies often feature intricate plots involving mistaken identities, disguises, and romantic entanglements, creating a sense of playful confusion and ultimately resolving in harmony and reconciliation.

"A Midsummer Night's Dream," for instance, intertwines the lives of four young lovers, a group of amateur actors, and the magical inhabitants of a forest, creating a fantastical world where reality and illusion blur. The play explores themes of love and transformation, highlighting the unpredictable and often irrational nature of human emotions. The use of magical elements and the interplay between the human and supernatural realms reflect Shakespeare's fascination with the complexities of the human psyche and the mysteries of the natural world.

While his comedies celebrate the joys and follies of human relationships, Shakespeare's tragedies delve into the darker aspects of the human condition, exploring themes of ambition, jealousy, revenge, and moral corruption. His great tragedies, including "Hamlet," "Othello," "King Lear," and "Macbeth," are among the most profound and influential works in the literary canon, offering timeless insights into the struggles and dilemmas that define the human experience.

"Hamlet," often considered Shakespeare's greatest play, is a profound exploration of grief, madness, and the search for truth and justice. The character of Prince Hamlet, with his complex psychological depth and existential musings, embodies the universal human quest for meaning and the difficulty of making ethical choices in a world rife with deceit and corruption. The play's famous soliloquy, "To be, or not to be," reflects Hamlet's inner turmoil and his contemplation of life and death, capturing the essence of human uncertainty and the desire for resolution.

"Othello," another of Shakespeare's masterpieces, examines the destructive power of jealousy and the tragic consequences of trusting appearances over reality. The character of Othello, a Moorish general in the Venetian army, is manipulated by the deceitful Iago, whose jealousy and resentment drive him to destroy Othello's life. The play's exploration of racial prejudice, manipulation, and the fragility of trust remains relevant today, offering a powerful commentary on the complexities of human relationships and the devastating effects of betrayal.

"King Lear" is a tragic tale of power, betrayal, and madness, centering on the aging King Lear, who divides his kingdom among his daughters, only to be betrayed by the two who professed the greatest love for him. The play's portrayal of Lear's descent into madness and his realization of the superficiality of worldly power and wealth offers a poignant meditation on the nature of authority, familial bonds, and the human capacity for suffering and redemption.

"Macbeth," one of Shakespeare's most intense and psychologically complex tragedies, explores the corrosive effects of unchecked ambition and the moral consequences of pursuing power at any cost. The character of Macbeth, a Scottish nobleman driven by prophecy and spurred on by his wife's ambition, descends into a spiral of murder, paranoia, and self-destruction. The play's depiction of guilt, fear, and the supernatural, along with its examination of the psychological effects of evil actions, provides a powerful exploration of the dark side of human nature.

In addition to his plays, Shakespeare's sonnets and narrative poems are celebrated for their lyrical beauty and profound insights into love, time, and mortality. His sonnet sequence, comprising 154 poems, delves into the complexities of love and desire, the passage of time, and the nature of art and beauty. Sonnets such as "Shall I compare thee to a summer's day?" (Sonnet 18) and "Let me not to the marriage of true minds" (Sonnet 116) are among the most famous and enduring poems in the English language, admired for their eloquence, emotional depth, and intricate wordplay.

Shakespeare's influence extends beyond literature into the realms of theater, film, and popular culture. His plays have been adapted into countless films, television shows, and modern retellings, demonstrating their enduring relevance and universal appeal. The themes and characters of his works continue to resonate with audiences, inspiring new interpretations and adaptations that explore the timeless questions and conflicts at the heart of the human experience.

The legacy of Shakespeare is not confined to his written works; his contributions to the English language are immense. He is credited with coining or popularizing hundreds of words and phrases that are still in use today, such as "bedazzled," "fashionable," "all that glitters is not gold," and "break the ice." His innovative use of language, including his skillful use of metaphor, simile, and wordplay, has enriched the English lexicon and influenced generations of writers and speakers.

Shakespeare's impact on theater is equally profound. His plays transformed the nature of drama, elevating it from simple entertainment to a sophisticated art form that explores the depths of human emotion and experience. His ability to create complex, multi-dimensional characters who grapple with moral dilemmas and existential questions set a new standard for dramatic characterization, influencing the development of modern drama and the way we understand and portray human behavior on stage.

Shakespeare's work also reflects a deep understanding of the human condition and a compassionate view of humanity's strengths and weaknesses. His characters, from the noble and heroic to the flawed and villainous, embody the full range of human emotions and experiences, offering a rich tapestry of the joys, sorrows, and complexities of life. His exploration of themes such as love, power, identity, and mortality continue to resonate with audiences, providing timeless insights into the challenges and triumphs of the human journey.

Despite his monumental achievements, much of Shakespeare's life remains shrouded in mystery. Little is known about his personal life, and scholars have long debated various aspects of his biography, including his religious beliefs, sexual orientation, and the true authorship of his works. Some have even questioned whether a single individual could have produced such a vast and diverse body of work, suggesting that Shakespeare may have been a front for a group of writers or a pseudonym for another author. However, the evidence supporting Shakespeare's authorship is compelling, and his identity as the Bard remains widely accepted.

Shakespeare's enduring legacy is a testament to his genius and the universal appeal of his work. His ability to capture the essence of the human experience in all its complexity, beauty, and tragedy has made him a central figure in the literary canon and a source of inspiration for artists, writers, and thinkers around the world. His works continue to be studied, performed, and celebrated, reflecting the timeless nature of his insights and the power of his artistry.

Chapter 4: Ludwig van Beethoven

Ludwig van Beethoven, born on December 17, 1770, in Bonn, Germany, is widely regarded as one of the greatest composers in the history of Western music. His life and work span the Classical and Romantic periods, and he is known for his revolutionary approach to music, which expanded the boundaries of composition and performance. Beethoven's legacy includes an extensive body of work that continues to influence musicians and composers to this day. His symphonies, concertos, piano sonatas, and string quartets are celebrated for their emotional depth, structural complexity, and innovative use of musical elements.

Beethoven's early life was marked by a combination of familial pressures and musical promise. His father, Johann van Beethoven, was a musician who recognized his son's prodigious talent and sought to turn him into a child prodigy similar to Wolfgang Amadeus Mozart. Johann's rigorous and often harsh training methods had a significant impact on young Ludwig, who showed an early aptitude for music. Despite the challenges at home, Beethoven's talent flourished, and he began to study with prominent musicians in Bonn, including Christian Gottlob Neefe, who introduced him to the works of Bach and Mozart.

In 1787, Beethoven traveled to Vienna, the cultural capital of Europe, where he briefly studied with Mozart. This visit marked a significant turning point in his musical development, although it was cut short by the death of his mother, which forced him to return to Bonn. Beethoven's formative years in Bonn were crucial to his development as a composer. He held various positions as a court musician and became familiar with the works of prominent composers, including Haydn and Mozart, whose influence would be evident in his early compositions.

In 1792, Beethoven moved to Vienna permanently, where he quickly gained a reputation as a virtuoso pianist and improviser. He studied with Joseph Haydn, one of the leading composers of the time, and later with Antonio Salieri and Johann Georg Albrechtsberger, who provided him with a solid foundation in composition. Vienna provided Beethoven with a stimulating environment where he could interact with other musicians and composers and gain exposure to the latest musical trends and innovations. His early years in Vienna were marked by a period of intense creativity and experimentation, during which he began to develop his unique musical voice.

Beethoven's early compositions, such as his Piano Trios, Op. 1, and the first two symphonies, show the influence of his classical predecessors, particularly Haydn and Mozart. These works adhere to the formal structures of the Classical period, including the sonata-allegro form and the use of balanced phrases and clear tonalities. However, even in these early works, one can detect Beethoven's emerging individuality and his tendency to push the boundaries of traditional forms. His early piano sonatas, for instance, are notable for their dramatic contrasts, bold harmonic explorations, and virtuosic demands, reflecting his exceptional skills as a pianist and his desire to expand the expressive possibilities of the instrument.

One of the defining features of Beethoven's music is its emotional intensity and depth. He was a master at conveying a wide range of emotions, from joy and triumph to despair and longing, and his music often reflects his personal struggles and triumphs. Beethoven's life was marked by numerous challenges, including his deteriorating hearing, which began to affect him in his late twenties. The realization that he was going deaf was a devastating blow to Beethoven, who feared that he would no longer be able to perform or compose music. This period of despair is poignantly captured in his "Heiligenstadt Testament," a letter he wrote to his brothers in 1802, in which he expressed his anguish and contemplated suicide. However, Beethoven ultimately resolved to continue composing, seeing his art as a means of transcending his suffering and achieving a higher purpose.

Beethoven's struggle with deafness profoundly influenced his music, leading him to explore new avenues of expression and to develop a more introspective and innovative style. His middle period, often referred to as his "heroic" period, is characterized by works that are grand in scale, rich in thematic development, and marked by a sense of struggle and triumph. During this period, Beethoven composed some of his most celebrated works, including the Third Symphony (the "Eroica"), the Fifth Symphony, and the Violin Concerto in D major. These works are notable for their dramatic contrasts, powerful rhythmic drive, and innovative use of orchestration, which expanded the possibilities of symphonic writing.

The "Eroica" Symphony, composed in 1803-1804, represents a turning point in Beethoven's career and a milestone in the history of Western music. Originally dedicated to Napoleon Bonaparte, whom Beethoven admired as a champion of liberty and equality, the symphony was later re-dedicated to "the memory of a great man" after Napoleon declared himself emperor. The "Eroica" broke new ground with its unprecedented length, complex structure, and emotional depth, and it marked the beginning of Beethoven's exploration of the symphony as a medium for profound and expansive musical expression. The first movement, with its heroic and triumphant themes, sets the stage for a journey through conflict and resolution, while the second movement, a funeral march, explores themes of loss and mourning. The symphony's finale, with its joyful and exuberant variations, celebrates the triumph of the human spirit.

Beethoven's Fifth Symphony, composed between 1804 and 1808, is one of the most famous and frequently performed symphonies in the world. Its opening motif, often described as "fate knocking at the door," is one of the most recognizable themes in classical music. The Fifth Symphony is a powerful example of Beethoven's ability to create a sense of drama and momentum through the use of rhythmic drive and dynamic contrasts. The symphony's progression from the dark and tumultuous opening movement to the triumphant and victorious finale reflects Beethoven's personal journey from despair to hope, and it has become a symbol of human resilience and determination.

In addition to his symphonies, Beethoven's middle period saw the creation of some of his most important chamber works, including the "Razumovsky" string quartets, the "Kreutzer" Sonata for violin and piano, and the "Waldstein" and "Appassionata" piano sonatas. These works are characterized by their bold harmonic explorations, intricate counterpoint, and expressive depth, and they represent a significant expansion of the traditional forms and genres of the Classical period. Beethoven's chamber music from this period reflects his ability to create intimate and profound musical dialogues between instruments, and it showcases his mastery of both lyrical and dramatic expression.

Beethoven's "heroic" period also included significant contributions to the genre of the piano concerto, with his Fourth and Fifth Piano Concertos standing out as landmarks of the concerto repertoire. The Fourth Piano Concerto, composed in 1805-1806, is notable for its lyrical and introspective qualities, particularly in the first movement, which opens with a gentle and expressive piano solo. The Fifth Piano Concerto, known as the "Emperor" Concerto, is a work of grand scale and virtuosity, with its majestic opening movement, lyrical slow movement, and exuberant finale. Both concertos demonstrate Beethoven's ability to integrate the solo instrument with the orchestra in a way that creates a cohesive and dynamic musical dialogue.

Beethoven's late period, which began around 1815, is marked by a profound introspection and a radical departure from the conventions of his time. During this period, he composed some of his most challenging and innovative works, including the late string quartets, the Missa Solemnis, and the Ninth Symphony. These works reflect Beethoven's deepening philosophical and spiritual concerns, as well as his desire to explore new musical forms and structures.

The late string quartets, composed between 1824 and 1826, are considered some of the most profound and complex works in the chamber music repertoire. These quartets are notable for their exploration of unconventional forms, intricate counterpoint, and profound emotional expression. The Op. 131 quartet, in particular, is a monumental work that consists of seven interconnected movements, each exploring a different emotional and musical landscape. The late quartets challenge traditional notions of form and structure, and they reflect Beethoven's relentless pursuit of artistic innovation and his willingness to push the boundaries of musical expression.

The Missa Solemnis, completed in 1823, is a monumental work that combines elements of the Mass with a deeply personal and philosophical exploration of faith and spirituality. The Missa Solemnis is notable for its grandeur, complexity, and emotional depth, and it represents a significant departure from the traditional liturgical Mass. Beethoven's setting of the text is highly dramatic and expressive, and it reflects his belief in the power of music to convey profound spiritual truths and to inspire a sense of awe and reverence.

The Ninth Symphony, composed between 1822 and 1824, is perhaps Beethoven's most famous and ambitious work. The symphony is notable for its inclusion of a choral finale, which sets Friedrich Schiller's "Ode to Joy" to music. The Ninth Symphony is a work of immense scope and vision, combining elements of the symphonic, choral, and operatic traditions in a way that had never been done before. The symphony's final movement, with its powerful message of universal brotherhood and joy, has become a symbol of hope and unity, and it continues to resonate with audiences around the world.

Beethoven's impact on music extends far beyond his compositions. His innovative approach to form, harmony, and orchestration set new standards for musical expression and paved the way for the Romantic composers who followed him. His willingness to push the boundaries of traditional forms and to explore new musical ideas inspired generations of composers to experiment with new approaches to composition and to seek out new ways of expressing themselves through music.

Beethoven's influence is also evident in his approach to the role of the composer and performer. He was one of the first composers to view music as a means of personal and artistic expression, rather than merely as a craft to be mastered. This shift in perspective had a profound impact on the way composers and musicians approached their work, and it helped to establish the concept of the composer as a visionary artist who could communicate profound truths through music.

Beethoven's legacy is further reflected in his impact on the development of the orchestra and the concert hall. His symphonies, with their expanded orchestration and dramatic use of dynamics and contrasts, set new standards for orchestral performance and helped to establish the symphony as a major form of musical expression. His innovations in the use of form and structure in his symphonies and other works also influenced the development of the concerto, sonata, and quartet, and they continue to shape the way these forms are approached by composers and performers today.

Despite his many challenges, including his struggle with deafness and his often tumultuous personal life, Beethoven's music continues to inspire and uplift listeners around the world. His ability to convey the full range of human emotion, from joy and triumph to despair and longing, has made his music timeless and universal. His commitment to artistic innovation and his belief in the power of music to transcend the limitations of the human condition have left an indelible mark on the history of music and on the hearts of those who continue to be moved by his work.

Chapter 5: Wolfgang Amadeus Mozart

Wolfgang Amadeus Mozart, born on January 27, 1756, in Salzburg, Austria, is widely considered one of the most prolific, influential, and remarkable composers in the history of Western classical music. His full name was Johannes Chrysostomus Wolfgangus Theophilus Mozart, but he preferred to be known simply as Wolfgang Amadeus Mozart. His extraordinary talent and prodigious output, spanning over 600 works across various musical genres, have cemented his place as a quintessential figure of the Classical period, and his music continues to enchant and inspire audiences and musicians worldwide.

Mozart's early life was marked by an exceptional musical aptitude that manifested at a very young age. He was the youngest of seven children, though only he and his sister, Maria Anna (nicknamed Nannerl), survived infancy. His father, Leopold Mozart, was a respected composer, violinist, and assistant concertmaster at the Salzburg court. Recognizing his son's extraordinary musical potential, Leopold dedicated himself to nurturing Wolfgang's talents. By the age of three, Mozart showed an uncanny ability to play the clavier, and by the age of five, he had already composed several small pieces, demonstrating a remarkable grasp of melody, harmony, and form.

Leopold was keenly aware of his son's genius and embarked on a series of extensive tours across Europe to showcase Wolfgang's prodigious talents. These tours, which began in 1762, were not only a means of gaining recognition but also an opportunity for young Mozart to be exposed to a wide variety of musical styles and influences. The family visited many of Europe's major cultural centers, including Munich, Paris, London, and Vienna. During these travels, Mozart met many influential musicians and composers, including Johann Christian Bach (the youngest son of Johann Sebastian Bach), whose music had a profound impact on the young composer.

Mozart's early compositions reveal a precocious mastery of various musical forms and genres. His first symphonies, composed when he was only eight years old, show a remarkable understanding of orchestration and form. These early works, while influenced by the prevailing styles of the time, already exhibit Mozart's distinctive melodic gift and his ability to create music that is both sophisticated and accessible. His early operas, such as "Apollo et Hyacinthus" and "Bastien und Bastienne," composed when he was just eleven and twelve, respectively, demonstrate his ability to write compelling vocal music that blends elements of both Italian and German operatic traditions.

In 1769, at the age of 13, Mozart was appointed Konzertmeister (concertmaster) at the court of Salzburg. This position allowed him to continue developing his compositional skills while gaining valuable experience as a performer and conductor. However, Mozart's ambition and desire for a broader audience led him to seek opportunities beyond Salzburg. In 1777, he embarked on a tour with his mother to explore potential employment in Mannheim and Paris. Although this journey did not result in a permanent position, it exposed him to new musical influences and deepened his understanding of contemporary styles.

One of the most significant periods in Mozart's career began in 1781 when he moved to Vienna, the cultural and musical capital of Europe. It was in Vienna that Mozart truly flourished as a composer, producing some of his most enduring and innovative works. The move to Vienna also marked a significant shift in his career, as he sought to establish himself as a freelance composer and performer rather than relying on the patronage of the aristocracy. This decision reflected a broader trend in the late 18th century, as composers began to seek greater independence and to cater to a growing public audience.

Mozart's time in Vienna was marked by a period of intense creativity and prolific output across a wide range of musical genres. His piano concertos, composed during this period, are particularly noteworthy for their combination of virtuosity, lyrical beauty, and structural innovation. Works such as the Piano Concertos No. 20 in D minor (K. 466), No. 21 in C major (K. 467), and No. 23 in A major (K. 488) exemplify Mozart's ability to integrate the solo instrument with the orchestra in a way that creates a dynamic and expressive dialogue. These concertos are celebrated for their memorable themes, intricate interplay between the piano and orchestra, and the depth of emotional expression they convey.

Mozart's symphonies from his Viennese period also represent significant contributions to the orchestral repertoire. His later symphonies, such as Symphony No. 40 in G minor (K. 550) and Symphony No. 41 in C major (K. 551), known as the "Jupiter," are masterpieces of form, melody, and orchestration. The Symphony No. 40, with its brooding and intense character, is one of the most dramatic and emotionally charged works in Mozart's output. The "Jupiter" Symphony, with its grand and majestic character, is a culmination of Mozart's symphonic writing, featuring a final movement that showcases his extraordinary contrapuntal skills through the use of a complex and brilliant fugue.

Opera was another area in which Mozart made significant and lasting contributions. His operas are celebrated for their dramatic insight, lyrical beauty, and innovative use of orchestration and vocal writing. Works such as "The Abduction from the Seraglio" (K. 384), "The Marriage of Figaro" (K. 492), "Don Giovanni" (K. 527), and "The Magic Flute" (K. 620) are cornerstones of the operatic repertoire and continue to be performed regularly around the world. "The Marriage of Figaro," with its intricate plot and rich characterizations, exemplifies Mozart's ability to combine comedy and drama in a way that reflects the complexities of human relationships. "Don Giovanni," with its darker themes of seduction and retribution, showcases Mozart's skill in blending dramatic intensity with moments of lyrical beauty and humor. "The Magic Flute," a Singspiel that combines spoken dialogue with singing, is notable for its use of Masonic symbolism and its exploration of themes such as love, enlightenment, and the triumph of good over evil.

In addition to his operatic and orchestral works, Mozart made significant contributions to the chamber music repertoire. His string quartets, such as the six "Haydn" Quartets (K. 387, 421, 428, 458, 464, and 465), are masterpieces of the genre, characterized by their sophisticated interplay between the instruments and their exploration of form and harmony. The String Quintet in G minor (K. 516) and the Clarinet Quintet in A major (K. 581) are also celebrated for their lyrical beauty and structural elegance. Mozart's chamber music reflects his ability to create music that is both intellectually rigorous and deeply expressive, and it continues to be admired for its balance of form and emotion.

Mozart's contributions to the world of keyboard music are equally significant. His piano sonatas, such as the Sonata in A major (K. 331) with its famous "Rondo alla Turca," and the Sonata in C minor (K. 457), are notable for their lyrical melodies, expressive range, and technical demands. His sets of variations, such as the "Ah vous dirai-je, Maman" Variations (K. 265), demonstrate his ingenuity in transforming simple themes into complex and imaginative works. Mozart's keyboard music is celebrated for its clarity of form, its expressive depth, and its ability to convey a wide range of emotions, from playful exuberance to profound introspection.

One of the most remarkable aspects of Mozart's music is its universality and timeless appeal. His ability to combine clarity of form with expressive depth has made his music accessible and engaging to listeners of all backgrounds and musical preferences. Mozart's melodies are often simple yet profound, capable of conveying a wide range of emotions with an economy of means. His harmonic language, while rooted in the conventions of the Classical period, is rich in color and complexity, allowing for subtle shifts in mood and expression. Mozart's use of form, whether in the sonata-allegro structure of his symphonies and concertos or the da capo aria form of his operas, demonstrates his mastery of musical architecture and his ability to create works that are both cohesive and dynamically engaging.

Despite his remarkable achievements, Mozart's life was marked by personal and financial difficulties. His decision to pursue a career as a freelance composer in Vienna led to periods of financial instability, and he often struggled to secure steady income from his compositions and performances. Mozart's personal life was also fraught with challenges, including the death of four of his six children in infancy and his own declining health in his later years. Despite these difficulties, Mozart continued to compose prolifically, producing some of his most profound and innovative works in the final years of his life.

Mozart's Requiem in D minor (K. 626), left unfinished at the time of his death on December 5, 1791, is one of his most enigmatic and poignant works. Commissioned by an anonymous patron, the Requiem is shrouded in mystery and has been the subject of much speculation and myth. Completed by Mozart's student Franz Xaver Süssmayr, the Requiem is a work of profound emotional depth and spiritual intensity, reflecting Mozart's deep sense of mortality and his preoccupation with themes of death and redemption. The Requiem's powerful choral writing, dramatic contrasts, and haunting melodies make it one of the most moving and enduring works in the choral repertoire.

Mozart's influence on subsequent generations of composers and musicians is immeasurable. His innovative approach to composition, his mastery of form and melody, and his ability to convey deep emotion through music have inspired countless composers, from Ludwig van Beethoven and Franz Schubert to Johannes Brahms and Gustav Mahler. Mozart's music continues to be a cornerstone of the classical repertoire, and his works are regularly performed and recorded by musicians around the world. His legacy extends beyond the concert hall, as his music has been used in a wide range of cultural contexts, from film and television to ballet and popular music.

In addition to his impact on music, Mozart's life and work have inspired a vast body of literature, scholarship, and artistic interpretation. His life story, with its blend of prodigious talent, personal struggles, and tragic early death, has captured the imagination of biographers, novelists, and filmmakers. Works such as Peter Shaffer's play "Amadeus," which was later adapted into an Academy Award-winning film, have helped to popularize Mozart's story and to introduce his music to new audiences. The enduring fascination with Mozart's life and music reflects his unique ability to connect with people across different cultures and generations, and his legacy continues to inspire and captivate audiences around the world.

Chapter 6: Vincent van Gogh

Vincent van Gogh, born on March 30, 1853, in Groot-Zundert, a small village in the southern Netherlands, is widely regarded as one of the most iconic and influential figures in Western art. Despite a life marked by personal turmoil, mental illness, and financial struggle, van Gogh's artistic legacy includes some of the most celebrated and enduring works of the late 19th century. His distinctive style, characterized by bold colors, dynamic brushwork, and emotive intensity, has made his paintings among the most recognizable and beloved in the history of art. Van Gogh's life and work continue to captivate and inspire people around the world, and his art is seen as a profound expression of the human condition.

Vincent Willem van Gogh was born into a family with deep religious and artistic roots. His father, Theodorus van Gogh, was a Protestant minister, and his mother, Anna Cornelia Carbentus, came from a family of bookbinders and artists. Vincent was the eldest of six surviving children, and his early life was marked by a sense of duty and piety instilled by his parents. The van Gogh family had connections to the art world; Vincent's uncles were art dealers, which would later influence his own career path. Despite this artistic heritage, Vincent's early years were characterized by academic struggle and a lack of direction, which contributed to a sense of isolation and uncertainty that would persist throughout his life.

At the age of 16, van Gogh began working for the art dealership Goupil & Cie, where his uncle Cent van Gogh was a partner. This position took him to various cities, including The Hague, London, and Paris, exposing him to a wide range of artistic styles and movements. His time in London was particularly significant, as he developed a deep appreciation for English culture and literature, as well as a love for the works of artists such as John Constable and John Everett Millais. However, despite his early success in the art business, van Gogh's temperament and intense emotional nature led to conflicts with his employers, and he was eventually dismissed from Goupil in 1876.

Following his departure from the art world, van Gogh experienced a period of deep spiritual searching and contemplation. He returned to the Netherlands and began studying theology with the aim of becoming a minister, like his father. Van Gogh's religious fervor and desire to help the less fortunate led him to work as a lay preacher in the impoverished coal-mining region of Borinage in Belgium. During this time, he lived in extreme poverty, sharing his meager resources with the miners and their families. His experiences in Borinage had a profound impact on him, deepening his empathy for the suffering and struggles of ordinary people. However, van Gogh's unorthodox approach to ministry, which included giving away his possessions and living in squalor, ultimately led to his dismissal from the church.

It was during his time in Borinage that van Gogh began to seriously consider a career as an artist. He believed that art could be a powerful means of expressing his deep emotional and spiritual convictions, and he hoped to create works that would bring comfort and inspiration to others. With the encouragement of his younger brother, Theo van Gogh, who was an art dealer in Paris, Vincent began to study drawing and painting in earnest. His early works, such as "The Potato Eaters" (1885), reflect his desire to depict the harsh realities of peasant life with authenticity and empathy. These early paintings, characterized by their dark palette and somber tones, show the influence of the Dutch masters such as Rembrandt and the Barbizon School of French landscape painters.

In 1886, van Gogh moved to Paris to live with his brother Theo, who provided him with both financial and emotional support. The Parisian art scene was vibrant and dynamic, offering van Gogh exposure to a wide range of contemporary artistic movements and styles. He became acquainted with the works of the Impressionists, including Claude Monet, Camille Pissarro, and Edgar Degas, as well as the emerging Post-Impressionist artists such as Paul Gauguin and Georges Seurat. The vibrant colors and innovative techniques of these artists had a profound impact on van Gogh, leading him to adopt a brighter palette and a more expressive style. His Parisian works, such as "Still Life: Vase with Twelve Sunflowers" (1888), reflect this newfound sense of color and light, as well as his growing confidence as an artist.

Van Gogh's time in Paris was also marked by personal struggles and bouts of mental illness. He experienced episodes of depression and anxiety, which were exacerbated by his intense work ethic and the pressures of life in a bustling city. Despite these challenges, his time in Paris was a period of significant artistic growth and experimentation. He absorbed influences from a wide range of sources, including Japanese woodblock prints, which he admired for their bold use of color and composition. This eclectic mix of influences can be seen in works such as "The Courtesan" (1887), which combines elements of Japanese art with van Gogh's distinctive style.

In 1888, seeking a quieter and more contemplative environment, van Gogh moved to the town of Arles in the south of France. The Provençal landscape, with its vivid colors and intense light, provided him with a rich source of inspiration, and his time in Arles was one of the most productive periods of his career. It was here that he created some of his most iconic works, including "The Starry Night" (1889), "Café Terrace at Night" (1888), and "The Bedroom" (1888). These paintings are characterized by their bold, swirling brushstrokes, vibrant colors, and a sense of emotional intensity that reflects van Gogh's inner turmoil and passion for life.

Van Gogh's stay in Arles was also marked by his ill-fated attempt to establish an artist's colony. He invited Paul Gauguin to join him, hoping to create a supportive and collaborative environment where artists could work together and inspire one another. However, their time together was fraught with conflict, culminating in a violent altercation in December 1888 that resulted in van Gogh severing part of his own ear. This incident marked the beginning of a period of intense psychological distress for van Gogh, who spent time in various hospitals and asylums in an attempt to manage his mental illness.

Despite his struggles, van Gogh continued to produce an astonishing amount of work during this period. His paintings from his time in the asylum at Saint-Paul-de-Mausole in Saint-Rémy-de-Provence, such as "Irises" (1889) and "Wheatfield with Cypresses" (1889), reflect his deep connection to the natural world and his desire to capture its beauty and vitality. These works are characterized by their bold use of color, dynamic compositions, and a sense of movement and energy that conveys van Gogh's intense emotional response to the landscape around him.

In 1890, van Gogh moved to the village of Auvers-sur-Oise, near Paris, to be closer to his brother Theo and to receive treatment from Dr. Paul Gachet, a physician who was sympathetic to artists and had an interest in their mental health. During his time in Auvers, van Gogh's work took on a new sense of urgency and intensity. He produced a series of powerful and emotive paintings, including "Portrait of Dr. Gachet" (1890), "Wheatfield with Crows" (1890), and "The Church at Auvers" (1890). These works reflect van Gogh's profound sense of isolation and his struggle to find peace and stability in his life.

On July 27, 1890, van Gogh suffered a fatal gunshot wound, which has been widely interpreted as a suicide. He died two days later, on July 29, at the age of 37. His brother Theo, who had been a constant source of support and encouragement throughout his life, died six months later. Van Gogh's death marked the tragic end of a life filled with artistic brilliance and personal suffering, but it also marked the beginning of his posthumous rise to fame and recognition.

In the years following his death, van Gogh's work gradually gained recognition and acclaim. His bold use of color, expressive brushwork, and emotional intensity resonated with a new generation of artists and art lovers, and he became a key figure in the development of modern art. His influence can be seen in the work of subsequent artists, such as the Fauves, the Expressionists, and the Abstract Expressionists, who were inspired by his innovative approach to color and form, as well as his willingness to explore the depths of human emotion through his art.

Van Gogh's legacy extends beyond his influence on the art world. His life and work have inspired a vast body of literature, scholarship, and popular culture. His letters, particularly those to his brother Theo, provide a deeply moving and intimate insight into his thoughts, struggles, and creative process. These letters reveal a man of profound sensitivity and intellect, whose commitment to his art was matched by a deep empathy for the suffering and beauty of the world around him. Van Gogh's life story, with its blend of genius, tragedy, and triumph, has captured the imagination of people around the world and has made him an enduring symbol of the artist's struggle for authenticity and expression.

Van Gogh's work continues to captivate and inspire audiences around the world. His paintings, with their vivid colors, dynamic compositions, and emotional intensity, offer a window into the complexities of the human condition and the beauty of the natural world. His legacy is celebrated in museums, galleries, and cultural institutions worldwide, and his work remains a source of inspiration and wonder for people of all ages and backgrounds. As we continue to explore and appreciate his art, Vincent van Gogh's legacy lives on, reminding us of the enduring power of creativity and the profound impact that one individual's vision and passion can have on the world.

Chapter 7: Pablo Picasso

Pablo Picasso, one of the most influential artists of the 20th century, was born on October 25, 1881, in Málaga, Spain. His full name, a tribute to various saints and relatives, is an early indicator of the grandiosity that would come to define his career. Picasso's father, Don José Ruiz y Blasco, was a painter and art teacher who recognized and nurtured his son's prodigious talent from a young age. By the age of seven, Picasso was already demonstrating an exceptional aptitude for drawing, and his father began formally training him in the basics of figure drawing and oil painting.

Picasso's early education took place in various art schools, including the School of Fine Arts in La Coruña, where his father was a professor. By the age of 13, Picasso had surpassed his father's abilities, prompting Don José to give up painting altogether. In 1895, the family moved to Barcelona, and Picasso was admitted to the prestigious La Llotja school of fine arts. His exceptional talent continued to flourish, and by the age of 16, he was sent to Madrid's Royal Academy of San Fernando. However, Picasso found the formal academic approach stifling and was more inspired by the city's vibrant cultural life and its collection of classical and modern art.

Picasso's early works, known as the Blue Period (1901-1904), are characterized by somber tones and themes of poverty and despair, reflecting his own struggles and the suicide of his friend, Carlos Casagemas. This period gave way to the Rose Period (1904-1906), marked by warmer colors and subjects such as circus performers, reflecting a more optimistic outlook as Picasso settled in Paris and became integrated into the city's bohemian lifestyle. His relationships with artists, poets, and writers in Montmartre were crucial in shaping his artistic vision.

A groundbreaking phase in Picasso's career began in 1907 with the creation of "Les Demoiselles d'Avignon," a work that challenged conventional perspectives and laid the groundwork for Cubism. Alongside Georges Braque, Picasso developed this radical new style, characterized by fragmented forms and multiple viewpoints. Cubism represented a departure from traditional techniques, emphasizing abstract forms over realistic representation. This collaboration with Braque was intense and productive, resulting in works that redefined the boundaries of art.

As Picasso's reputation grew, so did his experimentation with different styles and mediums. The Synthetic Cubism phase, starting around 1912, saw Picasso incorporating collage elements into his paintings, further blurring the lines between art and reality. He continued to innovate, moving beyond Cubism to embrace Neoclassicism and Surrealism in the 1920s and 1930s. These periods were marked by a return to classical forms and mythological themes, as well as an exploration of dream-like, fantastical imagery.

The Spanish Civil War deeply affected Picasso, leading to the creation of one of his most famous works, "Guernica" (1937). This monumental painting, depicting the bombing of the Basque town during the war, is a powerful anti-war statement and a testament to Picasso's political engagement. The work's stark black and white palette, fragmented forms, and haunting imagery convey the horror and chaos of war, making it one of the most poignant artistic responses to conflict.

Throughout his life, Picasso was also known for his prolific output and relentless creativity, producing an estimated 50,000 artworks, including paintings, drawings, sculptures, ceramics, prints, and textiles. His ability to constantly reinvent himself and explore new artistic territories is unparalleled. He worked across multiple styles simultaneously, never confining himself to a single artistic movement.

Picasso's personal life was as complex and dynamic as his art. He had numerous relationships with women who often served as muses and significantly influenced his work. His tumultuous love life included marriages, affairs, and partnerships with notable figures like Fernande Olivier, Olga Khokhlova, Marie-Thérèse Walter, Dora Maar, Françoise Gilot, and Jacqueline Roque. These relationships were often reflected in his art, with each woman bringing new inspiration and phases to his oeuvre.

In addition to his artistic contributions, Picasso's personality and public persona played a significant role in his enduring legacy. He was known for his charismatic and often contradictory nature, embodying both charm and ruthlessness. His interactions with fellow artists, writers, and intellectuals further cemented his status as a cultural icon.

Picasso's later years were marked by continued innovation and productivity. Even in his 70s and 80s, he continued to produce groundbreaking work, exploring themes of mortality and legacy. He remained active until his death on April 8, 1973, in Mougins, France. His passing marked the end of an era, but his influence on art and culture remains profound.

Picasso's impact on the art world is immeasurable. He challenged traditional notions of art, pushed the boundaries of creativity, and inspired countless artists across generations. His work not only reflects the tumultuous times in which he lived but also transcends them, offering timeless insights into the human condition. His legacy is preserved in numerous museums and collections worldwide, ensuring that his contributions to art and culture will be remembered and celebrated for generations to come.

Chapter 8: Marie Curie

Marie Curie, born Maria Skłodowska on November 7, 1867, in Warsaw, Poland, was a pioneering scientist whose work laid the foundations for significant advancements in physics and chemistry. Her early life was marked by intellectual rigor and a deep-seated resilience. Growing up in Russian-occupied Poland, Marie was the youngest of five children in a family that highly valued education. Her father, Władysław Skłodowski, was a mathematics and physics teacher, and her mother, Bronisława, managed a prestigious boarding school for girls. Despite facing financial difficulties and the oppressive political climate, the Skłodowska family fostered an environment that encouraged learning and critical thinking.

Marie demonstrated an early aptitude for mathematics and science, excelling in her studies at local schools. However, opportunities for higher education were limited for women in Poland at the time. Undeterred, Marie and her sister Bronisława made a pact to support each other's education. Marie worked as a governess and tutor, saving money to join Bronisława in Paris, where she could pursue her academic ambitions. In 1891, at the age of 24, Marie moved to Paris and enrolled at the Sorbonne, one of the few places in Europe where women could receive a rigorous scientific education.

At the Sorbonne, Marie immersed herself in her studies, earning degrees in physics and mathematics by 1894. During this period, she met Pierre Curie, a physicist whose research interests aligned with her own. The two married in 1895, forming one of the most remarkable scientific partnerships in history. Their collaboration led to groundbreaking discoveries in the field of radioactivity, a term coined by Marie herself. Inspired by the work of Henri Becquerel, who discovered that uranium emitted rays, the Curies sought to investigate the properties and potential applications of these mysterious emissions.

In 1898, the Curies announced the discovery of two new elements: polonium, named after Marie's homeland, and radium. These elements were found to be significantly more radioactive than uranium, leading to further investigations into their properties. The isolation of radium, in particular, was a monumental achievement that required processing tons of pitchblende, mineral rich in uranium, to extract minuscule amounts of radium chloride. This painstaking work, conducted under challenging conditions in makeshift laboratories, showcased Marie's extraordinary dedication and perseverance.

The significance of the Curies' work was recognized globally, culminating in the award of the Nobel Prize in Physics in 1903, which they shared with Henri Becquerel. Marie Curie became the first woman to receive a Nobel Prize, a testament to her exceptional contributions to science. However, the triumph was shadowed by personal and professional challenges. In 1906, Pierre Curie tragically died in a street accident, leaving Marie to continue their research alone while raising their two daughters, Irène and Ève.

Despite the profound loss, Marie's resolve never wavered. She took over Pierre's teaching position at the Sorbonne, becoming the institution's first female professor. Her research focused increasingly on the medical applications of radium, particularly in cancer treatment. In 1911, she was awarded a second Nobel Prize, this time in Chemistry, for her discovery of radium and polonium, and for her investigation of their properties. This unprecedented achievement cemented her legacy as a scientific trailblazer.

World War I saw Marie applying her expertise in radioactivity to develop mobile radiography units, known as "Little Curies," which were used to assist battlefield surgeons. She trained nurses and physicians in the use of X-ray equipment, significantly improving the treatment of wounded soldiers. This wartime effort highlighted her commitment to using science for humanitarian purposes.

Marie Curie's later years were marked by ongoing research and advocacy for scientific progress. She founded the Radium Institute (now the Curie Institute) in Paris, which became a major center for medical research. Her daughter Irène followed in her footsteps, contributing to advancements in nuclear science and also receiving a Nobel Prize in Chemistry alongside her husband, Frédéric Joliot-Curie, in 1935.

Marie Curie's impact extended beyond her scientific achievements. She broke barriers for women in science, challenging societal norms and inspiring generations of female scientists. Her perseverance in the face of personal hardship, her commitment to education and research, and her humanitarian efforts have left an indelible mark on history. Despite facing health issues likely caused by prolonged exposure to radiation, Curie continued her work until her death on July 4, 1934, from aplastic anemia.

Her legacy is preserved in numerous institutions and honors, including the element curium, named in her honor, and the Marie Curie Cancer Care charity in the UK, which continues to support cancer patients and their families. Marie Curie remains a symbol of scientific excellence and dedication, her life story a powerful reminder of the potential for human ingenuity and resilience to overcome formidable challenges and make lasting contributions to the world.

Chapter 9: Nikola Tesla

Nikola Tesla, born on July 10, 1856, in the village of Smiljan in the Austrian Empire (modern-day Croatia), was a visionary inventor and engineer whose contributions to science and technology continue to influence modern society. Tesla's early life was marked by a blend of intellectual curiosity and an insatiable quest for knowledge. His father, Milutin Tesla, was an Orthodox priest and writer, while his mother, Georgina Đuka Tesla, who had a talent for making home craft tools and memorizing long Serbian epic poems, was undoubtedly the source of Nikola's interest in inventing. From a young age, Tesla demonstrated remarkable abilities, such as memorizing entire books and performing complex mathematical calculations in his head.

Tesla's formal education began at the Higher Real Gymnasium in Karlovac, where he completed a four-year term in just three years, showcasing his extraordinary intellect. He later attended the Austrian Polytechnic in Graz, Austria, where he studied electrical engineering. Tesla was an exceptional student, known for his photographic memory and ability to grasp complex concepts quickly. However, he did not complete his degree due to a combination of financial difficulties and a falling out with one of his professors over the feasibility of the Gramme dynamo.

After leaving Graz, Tesla continued his studies informally, spending time at the University of Prague. During this period, he was deeply influenced by the works of physicist Heinrich Hertz, whose experiments with electromagnetic waves would later play a crucial role in Tesla's own work. Tesla's career took a significant turn in 1881 when he moved to Budapest to work for the Central Telephone Exchange. It was there, while walking in a park with a friend, that he conceived the idea for the rotating magnetic field, a fundamental principle behind alternating current (AC) systems. This breakthrough laid the groundwork for many of his future inventions.

In 1882, Tesla moved to Paris to work for the Continental Edison Company, where he gained practical experience in electrical engineering. Two years later, he emigrated to the United States, arriving in New York City with little more than a letter of recommendation to Thomas Edison. Tesla's work with Edison involved improving the efficiency of Edison's direct current (DC) motors and generators. Although Tesla successfully redesigned the equipment, resulting in significant improvements, he and Edison had conflicting views on the future of electrical power. Edison was a staunch advocate of direct current, while Tesla believed alternating current was more efficient and practical for long-distance power transmission.

The professional rift between Tesla and Edison culminated in Tesla leaving Edison's company. He then embarked on a partnership with George Westinghouse, who recognized the potential of Tesla's alternating current system. This collaboration sparked what became known as the "War of the Currents," a fierce competition between Edison's DC and Tesla's AC systems. Despite intense opposition and a campaign of misinformation led by Edison, Tesla's AC system ultimately prevailed, demonstrating its superiority through successful installations such as the 1893 World's Columbian Exposition in Chicago and the harnessing of Niagara Falls to generate hydroelectric power.

Tesla's inventions and theoretical work extended far beyond the realm of electrical power. He developed the Tesla coil, an electrical resonant transformer circuit that produces high-voltage, low-current, high-frequency alternating current electricity. The Tesla coil became the foundation for many radio and wireless transmission technologies. In addition, Tesla conducted pioneering work in wireless communication, envisioning a global system of wireless transmission of energy and information long before the advent of modern wireless technology. His experiments in Colorado Springs from 1899 to 1900 were particularly notable, as he achieved the wireless transmission of signals over a distance of 25 miles, lighting 200 lamps without wires and demonstrating the feasibility of wireless power.

One of Tesla's most ambitious projects was the Wardenclyffe Tower, a massive wireless transmission station located in Shoreham, New York. Funded initially by financier J.P. Morgan, the tower was intended to provide free wireless energy to the world. However, financial difficulties and the lack of continued funding led to the abandonment of the project in 1906, and the tower was eventually dismantled. Despite this setback, Tesla's vision of wireless energy transmission continues to inspire contemporary research in wireless power and communication.

Tesla's later years were marked by a series of inventions and patents, although many of his ideas were ahead of their time and not commercially viable. He explored diverse fields such as robotics, remote control, radar, and even theoretical concepts that anticipated the development of modern computers and smartphones. His work on bladeless turbines, known as Tesla turbines, demonstrated his ability to innovate across a wide range of technologies.

Despite his prodigious contributions to science and technology, Tesla struggled with financial instability throughout his life. He was often more interested in pursuing visionary ideas than in securing financial backing or commercial success. This led to periods of poverty and relative obscurity, particularly in his later years. Tesla was also known for his eccentricities, including his obsession with cleanliness, his aversion to pearls, and his tendency to work in isolation.

Tesla passed away on January 7, 1943, in New York City, leaving behind a legacy that would only be fully appreciated in the years following his death. Today, Tesla is celebrated as a pioneering genius whose work laid the foundations for numerous technological advancements. His contributions to the development of alternating current, radio, wireless communication, and many other fields have earned him a place among the greatest inventors and thinkers in history.

Tesla's influence extends beyond his inventions; he is also remembered for his visionary thinking and unwavering belief in the potential of science to transform the world. His life story, marked by triumphs and challenges, continues to inspire scientists, engineers, and innovators. Tesla's dedication to pushing the boundaries of what is possible serves as a reminder of the power of human ingenuity and the importance of daring to dream big. His legacy is preserved in numerous institutions, including the Nikola Tesla Museum in Belgrade, and his name endures as a symbol of innovation and creativity, inspiring new generations to explore the frontiers of science and technology.

Chapter 10: Thomas Edison

Thomas Edison, one of the most prolific inventors in history, was born on February 11, 1847, in Milan, Ohio. His parents, Samuel and Nancy Edison, played significant roles in his upbringing. Samuel was a versatile craftsman and shingle maker, while Nancy was a former schoolteacher who greatly influenced Edison's early education. Young Thomas, or "Al" as he was known, showed an early interest in mechanics and chemical experiments, fostering a lifelong curiosity that would lead to many groundbreaking inventions.

Edison's formal schooling was brief, lasting only a few months due to his perceived hyperactivity and difficulty focusing in a traditional classroom setting. His mother decided to homeschool him, recognizing his potential and nurturing his inquisitive nature. This personalized education allowed Edison to explore subjects that fascinated him, such as chemistry and physics. By the age of twelve, he had read scientific and technical books far beyond his years, and his curiosity about the world around him continued to grow.

At the age of 12, Edison took a job selling newspapers and snacks on the Grand Trunk Railroad, which connected Port Huron, Michigan, where his family had moved, to Detroit. This job not only provided him with income but also access to a broader array of scientific literature, thanks to the libraries he visited in larger cities. During this time, Edison set up a small laboratory in a baggage car, where he conducted experiments during the train's downtime. However, one of his chemical experiments caused a fire, leading to his dismissal from the job.

Edison's next venture was as a telegraph operator, a skill he had learned after saving a three-year-old boy from being struck by a runaway train. The boy's grateful father, a telegraph operator, taught Edison the trade. This period of his life was crucial, as it provided him with technical expertise and a deep understanding of electrical systems.

Edison's proficiency in telegraphy led to various positions across the United States and Canada, where he continued to invent and improve telegraph equipment.

In 1869, Edison moved to New York City and developed his first significant invention, the Universal Stock Ticker, which provided real-time stock prices to brokerage firms. This invention was a financial success and led to the establishment of his first laboratory and manufacturing facility in Newark, New Jersey. It was here that Edison began his systematic approach to invention, assembling a team of skilled workers and scientists to assist in his endeavors. This collaborative environment became a hallmark of his career and allowed for the rapid development of numerous innovations.

One of Edison's most notable achievements during this period was the development of the quadruplex telegraph, which could send two messages simultaneously in both directions on a single wire. This invention significantly improved the efficiency of telegraph communication and was quickly adopted by Western Union, the leading telegraph company at the time. Edison's ability to combine technical expertise with practical applications set the stage for his later successes.

In 1876, Edison moved his operations to Menlo Park, New Jersey, where he established a research laboratory that would become famous as the first industrial research lab in the world. It was in Menlo Park that Edison earned the nickname "The Wizard of Menlo Park." This facility allowed him to concentrate on multiple projects simultaneously and employ a larger team of skilled workers and scientists. The Menlo Park laboratory became the birthplace of some of Edison's most famous inventions.

One of Edison's most significant and enduring contributions was the development of the incandescent light bulb. While the concept of electric lighting had been explored by others, Edison's work was distinguished by his focus on creating a practical and long-lasting light bulb. After extensive experimentation with various materials, he discovered that a carbon filament could provide the necessary durability and efficiency. In 1879, Edison successfully demonstrated his light bulb, which could burn for up to 1200 hours, revolutionizing the way people illuminated their homes and workplaces. This breakthrough led to the establishment of the Edison Electric Light Company, which later became General Electric, one of the largest and most influential companies in the world.

Edison's invention of the light bulb was complemented by his development of the first electrical power distribution system. He recognized that for electric lighting to be widely adopted, there needed to be a reliable and efficient means of generating and distributing electricity. In 1882, Edison inaugurated the Pearl Street Station in New York City, the first commercial power plant, which provided electricity to a small section of Manhattan. This innovation laid the groundwork for modern electrical grids and transformed urban infrastructure.

Another area where Edison made significant contributions was sound recording. In 1877, he invented the phonograph, a device that could record and reproduce sound. This invention was initially met with skepticism, as many could not fathom the idea of recorded sound. However, Edison's phonograph became immensely popular and had a profound impact on the music industry and entertainment. The phonograph evolved over time, leading to the development of records and record players, which became household staples in the 20th century.

Edison's work in motion pictures also had a lasting impact. He developed the kinetoscope, an early motion picture device, and established the Edison Studios, where some of the first films were produced. Although Edison did not invent motion pictures, his contributions to the technology and industry were significant, helping to shape the future of cinema. The kinetoscope provided the foundation for future advancements in motion picture technology and the eventual rise of the film industry.

Throughout his career, Edison was awarded 1,093 U.S. patents and many more worldwide, a testament to his prolific output and diverse range of interests. His inventions spanned various fields, including telecommunications, electric power, sound recording, and motion pictures. Edison's ability to identify practical applications for scientific discoveries and his relentless pursuit of innovation set him apart as a leading figure in the Industrial Revolution.

Despite his many successes, Edison faced numerous challenges and controversies. His rivalry with Nikola Tesla is one of the most well-known aspects of his career. The "War of the Currents" between Edison's direct current (DC) and Tesla's alternating current (AC) systems was a fierce competition that ultimately saw Tesla's AC system prevail due to its greater efficiency and ability to transmit electricity over long distances. Edison's staunch support for DC and his efforts to discredit AC, including public demonstrations of its dangers, are often criticized as examples of his competitive and sometimes ruthless nature.

Edison's personal life was marked by both triumphs and tragedies. He married Mary Stilwell in 1871, and the couple had three children. After Mary's death in 1884, Edison married Mina Miller in 1886, and they had three more children. Despite his demanding work schedule, Edison maintained close relationships with his family and was known for his boundless energy and enthusiasm.

Thomas Edison passed away on October 18, 1931, in West Orange, New Jersey. His death marked the end of an era of unprecedented innovation and industrial growth. Edison's legacy endures through his numerous inventions and the impact they have had on modern society. He is remembered as a pioneering inventor whose work transformed daily life and set the stage for future technological advancements.

Edison's approach to invention, characterized by meticulous experimentation, teamwork, and a focus on practical applications, continues to influence the fields of science and engineering. His Menlo Park and West Orange laboratories are preserved as historic sites, symbolizing the birthplace of modern innovation. Edison's contributions to electric power, sound recording, and motion pictures remain foundational elements of contemporary technology and culture.

In addition to his technical achievements, Edison's entrepreneurial spirit and ability to commercialize his inventions were crucial to his success. He understood the importance of creating systems and infrastructures that supported his innovations, ensuring their widespread adoption and enduring impact. This blend of inventive genius and business acumen made Edison a pivotal figure in the transition from an agrarian to an industrial society.

Edison's story is not just one of individual brilliance but also of the collaborative efforts that drove his many successes. He surrounded himself with talented individuals who shared his vision and worked tirelessly to bring his ideas to life. This model of teamwork and innovation continues to inspire modern research and development practices.

Thomas Edison's life and work embody the spirit of American ingenuity and the relentless pursuit of progress. His legacy is a testament to the power of creativity, perseverance, and the transformative impact of technology on human life. As we continue to build on the foundations he laid, Edison's contributions remain a guiding light for future generations of inventors and innovators.

Chapter 11: Albert Einstein

Albert Einstein, one of the most influential scientists in history, was born on March 14, 1879, in Ulm, in the Kingdom of Württemberg in the German Empire. His parents, Hermann and Pauline Einstein, were secular, middle-class Jews. Hermann was an engineer and a salesman, while Pauline ran the household and took care of Albert and his younger sister, Maja. The Einstein family moved to Munich when Albert was a year old. There, Hermann and his brother Jakob founded a company that manufactured electrical equipment, which exposed young Albert to the principles of science and engineering at an early age.

Einstein's early education did not immediately reveal his exceptional intellectual capabilities. He spoke late and was thought by some to be slow. However, he displayed a deep curiosity about the natural world and an extraordinary ability to understand complex concepts. His interest in mathematics and science was piqued by a compass given to him by his father when he was five. The mysterious power that directed the needle fascinated him, sparking a lifelong passion for understanding the laws governing the universe.

Despite his intellectual curiosity, Einstein struggled with the rigid and rote educational methods of his time. He attended the Luitpold Gymnasium in Munich, where he often clashed with teachers and felt stifled by the authoritarian teaching style. His independent and inquisitive nature made him question traditional authority and seek knowledge outside the classroom. At home, Einstein's mother encouraged his musical development, and he became an accomplished violinist, finding solace and inspiration in music throughout his life.

In 1894, the Einstein family moved to Italy after their business failed. Albert remained in Munich to finish his schooling but grew increasingly unhappy and eventually left to join his family in Italy. Recognizing his son's dissatisfaction with the formal education system,

Hermann Einstein arranged for Albert to attend the Swiss Federal Polytechnic in Zurich. However, Albert first had to complete his secondary education. He enrolled in the Aargau Cantonal School in Aarau, Switzerland, where he thrived in a more liberal and supportive academic environment. It was here that he developed a clearer sense of his intellectual strengths and decided to pursue a career in physics.

Einstein graduated from the Polytechnic in 1900 with a diploma in mathematics and physics. Despite his academic achievements, he struggled to find a teaching position and spent two frustrating years working as a tutor and temporary teacher. In 1902, he secured a job at the Swiss Patent Office in Bern, where he evaluated patent applications for electromagnetic devices. This job, though unrelated to his academic aspirations, provided him with financial stability and ample free time to think and conduct research.

The period from 1902 to 1909, often referred to as Einstein's "miracle years," was marked by extraordinary productivity. In 1905, he published four groundbreaking papers in the "Annalen der Physik," which fundamentally transformed the understanding of physics. The first paper explained the photoelectric effect, demonstrating that light could be understood as quanta of energy, later called photons. This work provided crucial evidence for quantum theory and earned him the Nobel Prize in Physics in 1921.

Einstein's second paper of 1905 developed the theory of Brownian motion, providing empirical evidence for the existence of atoms and molecules, which were still debated at the time. His statistical analysis of the random movement of particles suspended in a fluid confirmed the predictions of atomic theory and advanced the field of statistical mechanics.

The third paper introduced the special theory of relativity, which revolutionized the concepts of space and time. Einstein postulated that the laws of physics are the same for all non-accelerating observers and that the speed of light is constant, regardless of the observer's frame of reference. This theory led to the famous equation $E=mc2E = mc^2E=mc2$, which established the equivalence of mass and energy and laid the groundwork for modern nuclear physics.

The fourth paper of 1905 dealt with the equivalence of mass and energy, presenting a more comprehensive understanding of the relationship between the two. These publications not only established Einstein as a leading theoretical physicist but also transformed the landscape of modern physics.

In 1909, Einstein left the Patent Office and began his academic career, accepting a position as an associate professor at the University of Zurich. His reputation as a brilliant physicist grew, and he held various academic posts in Europe, including positions at the Charles University in Prague and the Swiss Federal Institute of Technology in Zurich. In 1914, he was appointed director of the Kaiser Wilhelm Institute for Physics in Berlin and became a professor at the Humboldt University of Berlin.

During this period, Einstein developed the general theory of relativity, a more comprehensive theory that extended his special theory to include gravity. Published in 1915, the general theory of relativity proposed that gravity is not a force between masses but a curvature of space-time caused by mass and energy. This theory predicted the bending of light by gravity, a phenomenon confirmed during a solar eclipse in 1919, catapulting Einstein to international fame.

Einstein's prominence extended beyond the scientific community. His advocacy for civil rights, pacifism, and Zionism made him a public figure and a voice for social justice. As a Jew, he faced increasing hostility in Germany, especially with the rise of the Nazi regime. In 1933, following Hitler's ascent to power, Einstein emigrated to the United States, accepting a position at the Institute for Advanced Study in Princeton, New Jersey.

In the United States, Einstein continued his scientific work, focusing on unified field theory, an attempt to unify the fundamental forces of nature into a single theoretical framework. Although he did not succeed in this endeavor, his contributions to theoretical physics continued to inspire and challenge scientists.

Einstein's involvement in social and political issues also intensified. He spoke out against fascism, advocated for civil liberties, and supported the establishment of the State of Israel. Despite his pacifist beliefs, he signed a letter to President Franklin D. Roosevelt in 1939, warning of the potential for Nazi Germany to develop atomic weapons and urging the United States to initiate its own nuclear research. This letter contributed to the establishment of the Manhattan Project, which developed the atomic bomb during World War II. However, Einstein later expressed regret over his role in the development of nuclear weapons and became an advocate for nuclear disarmament.

Einstein's personal life was complex and marked by both successes and struggles. He married Mileva Marić, a fellow physics student, in 1903, and they had two sons, Hans Albert and Eduard. The marriage, however, was troubled, and they divorced in 1919. Later that year, Einstein married his cousin Elsa Löwenthal, who provided him with companionship and support until her death in 1936. Despite his fame and achievements, Einstein remained a humble and approachable individual, known for his sense of humor and simple lifestyle.

Einstein passed away on April 18, 1955, in Princeton, New Jersey. His death marked the end of an era in theoretical physics, but his legacy lives on through his groundbreaking contributions to science and his enduring influence on our understanding of the universe. His theories continue to be validated by experimental evidence and have paved the way for numerous technological advancements, including GPS systems, which rely on the principles of relativity.

Einstein's intellectual achievements are matched by his philosophical reflections on science, humanity, and the pursuit of knowledge. He believed in the power of curiosity and imagination, famously stating, "Imagination is more important than knowledge. For knowledge is limited, whereas imagination embraces the entire world, stimulating progress, giving birth to evolution." This perspective underscores the importance of creativity in scientific discovery and innovation.

Einstein's impact extends beyond his scientific contributions. He was a vocal advocate for peace, social justice, and human rights, using his platform to address global issues and promote ethical responsibility. His correspondence with world leaders, scientists, and public figures reveals a deep commitment to improving the human condition and fostering a more just and compassionate world.

In recognition of his extraordinary contributions, numerous honors and awards have been bestowed upon Einstein posthumously. His name has become synonymous with genius and scientific brilliance. Institutions, awards, and even a unit of measurement, the Einstein (a measure of light energy), are named in his honor. His intellectual legacy continues to inspire scientists, educators, and students worldwide, encouraging the pursuit of knowledge and the exploration of the mysteries of the universe.

Einstein's life and work exemplify the power of human intellect and creativity to transform our understanding of the natural world. His theories of relativity revolutionized physics, while his insights into quantum mechanics laid the groundwork for future discoveries. His philosophical reflections on science and society challenge us to consider the broader implications of our knowledge and actions, fostering a sense of ethical responsibility and global citizenship.

Albert Einstein remains a towering figure in the history of science, his contributions shaping the course of modern physics and influencing a wide range of disciplines. His legacy is a testament to the enduring power of curiosity, imagination, and the relentless pursuit of truth, inspiring future generations to explore the unknown and unlock the secrets of the universe.

Chapter 12: Frida Kahlo

Frida Kahlo, born Magdalena Carmen Frida Kahlo y Calderón on July 6, 1907, in Coyoacán, Mexico City, is one of the most iconic and influential artists of the 20th century. Her life and work have captivated audiences worldwide, making her a symbol of resilience, feminism, and artistic genius. Kahlo's unique style and personal narrative have solidified her place in the annals of art history.

Kahlo was born to a German father, Guillermo Kahlo, and a Mexican mother, Matilde Calderón y González. Her father was a photographer who had a significant influence on her life, instilling in her a sense of discipline and an appreciation for the arts. Kahlo's childhood was marked by illness and physical challenges. At the age of six, she contracted polio, which left her right leg thinner and shorter than her left. This condition caused her to limp and affected her self-esteem, but it also fostered her determination and resilience.

In 1922, Kahlo enrolled in the prestigious National Preparatory School in Mexico City, one of the few institutions that admitted women at the time. There, she became involved with a group of politically and intellectually active students known as the "Cachuchas." This group included future Mexican intellectuals and political leaders. It was during this period that Kahlo first encountered Diego Rivera, a prominent Mexican muralist who would later become her husband. Rivera was working on a mural at the school, and Kahlo was captivated by his artistic prowess and revolutionary ideals.

Kahlo's initial career aspirations were not in the arts but in medicine. She was an excellent student, passionate about biology and anatomy, and aimed to become a doctor. However, her life took a dramatic turn on September 17, 1925, when she was involved in a horrific bus accident. The accident resulted in multiple fractures to her spine, pelvis, collarbone, and ribs, as well as other severe injuries. She endured numerous surgeries and spent months bedridden, in constant pain. During her lengthy recovery, Kahlo turned to painting as a means of coping with her physical and emotional suffering.

Confined to her bed, Kahlo began painting self-portraits using a special easel that allowed her to paint while lying down. Her early works were deeply personal, reflecting her pain and vulnerability. Kahlo once said, "I paint myself because I am so often alone and because I am the subject I know best." This introspective approach became a defining characteristic of her art. Her self-portraits are raw, unflinching examinations of her identity, her physical suffering, and her emotional turmoil.

In 1929, Kahlo married Diego Rivera. Their relationship was tumultuous, characterized by passionate love and mutual infidelity. Rivera was twenty years her senior and already an established artist, while Kahlo was still developing her style and gaining recognition. Despite their differences and frequent conflicts, Rivera and Kahlo shared a deep bond and mutual respect for each other's work. Rivera recognized Kahlo's talent and encouraged her to pursue her art seriously. He once remarked that Frida was "the greatest artist of the century."

Kahlo and Rivera's marriage was marked by numerous separations and reconciliations, but their partnership profoundly influenced Kahlo's work. Rivera's support and encouragement played a crucial role in her artistic development, and she often credited him with helping her find her voice as an artist. Kahlo's work during this period began to reflect a fusion of traditional Mexican folk art and modernist influences, creating a unique and distinctive style.

Kahlo's art is characterized by its vivid colors, bold imagery, and symbolic content. Her work often incorporates elements of Mexican culture, including indigenous traditions, religious iconography, and folk motifs. She drew inspiration from the rich visual culture of Mexico, blending these influences with her personal experiences and emotions. Kahlo's paintings are deeply autobiographical, exploring themes of identity, gender, pain, and mortality.

One of Kahlo's most famous works is "The Two Fridas" (1939), a large-scale double self-portrait that reflects her inner turmoil and dual heritage. In the painting, two versions of Kahlo sit side by side, holding hands. One Frida is dressed in traditional Tehuana clothing, representing her Mexican heritage, while the other wears a European-style dress, symbolizing her mixed ancestry. The painting also depicts Kahlo's physical and emotional pain, with visible veins connecting the two hearts. "The Two Fridas" is a powerful exploration of Kahlo's complex identity and the conflicting aspects of her personality.

Another significant work is "Self-Portrait with Thorn Necklace and Hummingbird" (1940). In this painting, Kahlo portrays herself with a thorn necklace that pierces her skin, drawing blood. A dead hummingbird hangs from the necklace, and behind her, a black cat and a monkey stare intently. The painting is rich with symbolism, reflecting Kahlo's suffering, her connection to nature, and her resilience. The thorn necklace represents the pain she endured, while the hummingbird and animals symbolize aspects of her identity and emotional state.

Kahlo's paintings often include elements of surrealism, although she never fully identified with the movement. Her work was deeply personal and rooted in her own experiences, rather than the exploration of the unconscious mind that characterized much of surrealist art. Nevertheless, her dreamlike imagery and symbolic content have led many to associate her with surrealism. Kahlo herself rejected this label, stating, "They thought I was a surrealist, but I wasn't. I never painted dreams. I painted my own reality."

Kahlo's art gained international recognition during her lifetime, although she struggled with physical pain and health issues throughout her career. She exhibited her work in Mexico, the United States, and

Europe, earning acclaim and admiration from critics and fellow artists. In 1938, she had her first solo exhibition at the Julien Levy Gallery in New York City, which was a significant success. The following year, she traveled to Paris for an exhibition organized by André Breton, a leading figure in the surrealist movement. During her time in Paris, Kahlo met many influential artists, including Pablo Picasso and Marcel Duchamp, further cementing her reputation as a significant figure in the art world.

Despite her artistic achievements, Kahlo's health continued to deteriorate. She underwent numerous surgeries and medical treatments, and her mobility was severely limited. Her chronic pain and physical suffering were constant companions, and she often depicted her struggles in her art. Despite these challenges, Kahlo remained fiercely determined and continued to paint, even from her hospital bed.

In the 1940s and 1950s, Kahlo's work began to receive greater recognition in her home country. She became a member of the Seminario de Cultura Mexicana, a prestigious cultural organization, and taught at the Escuela Nacional de Pintura, Escultura y Grabado "La Esmeralda" in Mexico City. Her influence on a younger generation of Mexican artists was profound, and she became a celebrated figure in the Mexican art community.

Kahlo's final years were marked by increasing physical pain and declining health. In 1953, she had her first solo exhibition in Mexico at the Galería Arte Contemporáneo. Despite her frailty, she attended the opening in a bed, transported by ambulance, demonstrating her unwavering dedication to her art. This exhibition was a significant moment in her career, bringing her work to a wider audience in her homeland.

Frida Kahlo passed away on July 13, 1954, at the age of 47, in her beloved Blue House (La Casa Azul) in Coyoacán. Her death was a great loss to the art world, but her legacy continued to grow in the decades that followed. The Blue House was later converted into the

Frida Kahlo Museum, preserving her memory and her contributions to art and culture.

In the years since her death, Kahlo's work has gained widespread recognition and acclaim. She has become a global icon, celebrated for her artistic achievements and her role as a feminist and cultural symbol. Her life and art have inspired countless books, documentaries, and films, cementing her status as a legendary figure in art history.

Kahlo's influence extends beyond the art world. She has become a symbol of resilience and empowerment for women and marginalized groups. Her unapologetic self-expression and refusal to conform to societal norms resonate with those who seek to challenge conventional expectations and embrace their true selves.

Kahlo's work continues to be exhibited in major museums and galleries around the world, and her paintings fetch record prices at auctions. Her distinctive style, characterized by bold colors, symbolic imagery, and a deep connection to her cultural heritage, remains instantly recognizable and continues to captivate audiences.

In recent years, there has been a renewed interest in Kahlo's life and work, with numerous exhibitions, publications, and retrospectives dedicated to her legacy. Her influence can be seen in contemporary art, fashion, and popular culture, reflecting her enduring impact on the world.

Frida Kahlo's story is one of extraordinary talent, resilience, and passion. Her ability to transform personal pain into powerful and evocative art has left an indelible mark on the history of art. As a woman who defied societal expectations and embraced her unique identity, Kahlo's legacy continues to inspire and empower future generations. Her life and work remind us of the transformative power of art and the enduring strength of the human spirit.

Chapter 13: Virginia Woolf

Virginia Woolf, born Adeline Virginia Stephen on January 25, 1882, in London, England, is celebrated as one of the most innovative and influential writers of the 20th century. Her novels, essays, and non-fiction works have left an indelible mark on literature and feminist thought. Woolf's life and career were marked by profound creativity, intellectual rigor, and a deep engagement with the complexities of human experience.

Virginia was born into a distinguished literary and intellectual family. Her father, Sir Leslie Stephen, was a prominent historian, author, and critic, while her mother, Julia Prinsep Stephen, was a renowned beauty and philanthropist. The Stephen household was a hub of intellectual activity, frequented by notable writers, artists, and thinkers of the time. This stimulating environment fostered Woolf's early interest in literature and writing.

Woolf's childhood was also marked by personal tragedy. Her mother died when Virginia was just thirteen, and her half-sister Stella Duckworth, who had taken on the maternal role, passed away two years later. These losses profoundly affected Woolf, contributing to her lifelong struggle with mental health issues. Despite these challenges, she was a voracious reader and began to write from a young age, displaying a keen literary talent.

The Stephen family spent their summers at Talland House in St. Ives, Cornwall, which would later become the setting for Woolf's novel "To the Lighthouse." These idyllic retreats provided Virginia with a deep connection to nature and the sea, themes that would recur in her writing. The death of her father in 1904 prompted the Stephen siblings to move to the Bloomsbury district of London, where they established a new home and began to form what would become the Bloomsbury Group.

The Bloomsbury Group was an influential collective of writers, artists, and intellectuals, including figures such as Lytton Strachey, John Maynard Keynes, E.M. Forster, and Roger Fry. This group challenged Victorian norms and championed modernist ideas in art and literature. Woolf thrived in this environment, finding both intellectual stimulation and emotional support among her peers. The Bloomsbury Group's emphasis on personal freedom, artistic experimentation, and sexual liberation profoundly influenced Woolf's writing and worldview.

In 1912, Virginia married Leonard Woolf, a political theorist and writer. Their marriage was a partnership of intellectual equals, and Leonard provided Virginia with the stability and support she needed to pursue her writing. Together, they founded the Hogarth Press in 1917, a small publishing house that allowed them to publish experimental and avant-garde works, including Virginia's own writings. The Hogarth Press played a crucial role in the dissemination of modernist literature, publishing works by T.S. Eliot, Katherine Mansfield, and Sigmund Freud, among others.

Woolf's early novels, "The Voyage Out" (1915) and "Night and Day" (1919), received modest attention, but it was her subsequent works that established her as a pioneering literary figure. "Jacob's Room" (1922) marked a departure from traditional narrative forms, experimenting with stream-of-consciousness techniques and fragmented perspectives. This novel was followed by "Mrs. Dalloway" (1925), which solidified Woolf's reputation as a leading modernist writer. "Mrs. Dalloway" explores a single day in the life of Clarissa Dalloway, interweaving her thoughts and experiences with those of other characters, creating a rich tapestry of interconnected lives and inner worlds.

Woolf's innovative narrative techniques and psychological depth reached new heights in "To the Lighthouse" (1927), widely regarded as her masterpiece. The novel is structured in three parts, with a significant temporal gap between the first and second sections. This structure allows Woolf to explore themes of time, memory, and the impermanence of human experience. "To the Lighthouse" is also a deeply personal work, drawing on Woolf's own childhood memories and her complex relationship with her parents.

In "Orlando: A Biography" (1928), Woolf experimented with the genre of biography, blending historical fiction and fantasy. The novel traces the life of its protagonist, Orlando, who changes sex from male to female and lives for several centuries. "Orlando" is a playful and provocative exploration of gender identity and the fluidity of human experience. The novel was inspired by Woolf's close relationship with Vita Sackville-West, a fellow writer and member of the Bloomsbury Group.

Woolf's feminist convictions are most explicitly articulated in her essay "A Room of One's Own" (1929). Based on a series of lectures she delivered at women's colleges, the essay argues that women must have financial independence and personal space to create literature. Woolf examines the historical exclusion of women from intellectual and artistic pursuits and advocates for a reimagining of the literary canon to include female voices. "A Room of One's Own" remains a foundational text in feminist literary criticism and has inspired generations of women writers and thinkers.

Woolf continued to explore themes of gender, power, and creativity in "The Waves" (1931), a novel composed of soliloquies spoken by six characters. The novel's structure mimics the ebb and flow of the sea, creating a rhythmic and poetic meditation on the nature of identity and consciousness. "The Waves" is considered one of Woolf's most experimental works, showcasing her mastery of language and narrative form.

In addition to her novels, Woolf was a prolific essayist and critic. Her essays, collected in volumes such as "The Common Reader" (1925, 1932), demonstrate her keen insights into literature and culture.

Woolf's critical writings are characterized by their elegance, wit, and depth of analysis, offering readers a window into her intellectual world. Her essay "Modern Fiction" (1925) outlines her vision for a new kind of literature that captures the complexities of modern life, breaking away from the constraints of traditional realism.

Woolf's personal life was marked by periods of intense creativity and profound despair. She experienced recurrent episodes of severe depression and mental illness, exacerbated by the trauma of her early losses and the pressures of her literary career. Despite her struggles, Woolf remained committed to her writing, finding solace and expression in her work. Her letters and diaries, published posthumously, provide intimate insights into her thoughts, emotions, and creative process.

During the 1930s, Woolf's writing took on a more overtly political tone, reflecting her growing concern with the rise of fascism and the threat of war. "The Years" (1937) and "Three Guineas" (1938) address issues of social justice, education, and the role of women in society. In "Three Guineas," Woolf examines the connections between patriarchy, militarism, and the suppression of women's rights, advocating for a more just and equitable world.

The outbreak of World War II and the subsequent bombing of London deeply affected Woolf. Her final novel, "Between the Acts" (1941), reflects the sense of dislocation and uncertainty of the time, exploring themes of history, art, and the collective unconscious. The novel was published posthumously, as Woolf's life came to a tragic end in 1941.

On March 28, 1941, overwhelmed by her mental illness and the devastation of the war, Woolf filled her pockets with stones and walked into the River Ouse near her home in Sussex. Her body was found three weeks later. In her final letter to Leonard, she expressed her love and gratitude, acknowledging that she could no longer endure the torment of her mental illness. Woolf's death was a great loss to literature, but her legacy endures through her profound and innovative contributions to the literary canon.

Virginia Woolf's work continues to inspire and challenge readers, writers, and scholars. Her exploration of consciousness, her innovative narrative techniques, and her commitment to feminist ideals have left a lasting impact on literature and culture. Woolf's life and work remind us of the transformative power of art and the importance of intellectual and creative freedom.

In the years since her death, Woolf's influence has only grown. Her works have been translated into numerous languages, and she is widely studied in academic settings. Woolf's novels, essays, and diaries offer rich and multifaceted perspectives on the human condition, making her a timeless and essential figure in literary history.

Woolf's legacy is also evident in the ongoing relevance of her ideas about gender, identity, and creativity. Her call for women's financial independence and personal space resonates strongly in contemporary discussions about gender equality and the representation of women in the arts. Woolf's belief in the necessity of creative freedom and her critique of societal constraints continue to inspire new generations of writers and thinkers.

Virginia Woolf's life and work embody the complexities and contradictions of the human experience. Her ability to capture the nuances of consciousness and emotion, her innovative narrative techniques, and her commitment to social justice and feminist ideals make her a truly remarkable and enduring figure in the world of literature. Through her writing, Woolf invites us to explore the depths of our own minds and to challenge the boundaries of what is possible in art and life.

Chapter 14: James Joyce

James Joyce, born James Augustine Aloysius Joyce on February 2, 1882, in Dublin, Ireland, is widely regarded as one of the most influential and innovative writers of the 20th century. His work, characterized by its experimental style and intricate exploration of the human psyche, has left an indelible mark on modernist literature. Joyce's life and writings reflect a profound engagement with the cultural, social, and political complexities of his time.

Joyce was born into a middle-class Catholic family, the eldest of ten surviving children. His father, John Stanislaus Joyce, was a talented singer and a fervent supporter of Irish nationalism, but his financial mismanagement and alcoholism led the family into financial instability. His mother, Mary Jane Murray, was a devout Catholic who played a significant role in Joyce's early religious education. The young Joyce showed early promise as a student, excelling academically and displaying a precocious talent for languages and literature.

Joyce's education began at the Clongowes Wood College, a Jesuit boarding school, where he developed a lifelong ambivalence toward Catholicism. The rigorous religious instruction he received there left a lasting impression on him, both in his critical attitude towards organized religion and his deep appreciation for its ritualistic and symbolic aspects. Joyce later attended Belvedere College, another Jesuit institution, and then University College Dublin, where he studied modern languages.

During his university years, Joyce became increasingly involved in the literary and intellectual circles of Dublin. He published his first critical essay, "The Day of the Rabblement," in 1901, which criticized the Irish Literary Theatre for its conservative approach and called for more innovative and challenging works. This essay marked the beginning of Joyce's career as a writer and his commitment to artistic experimentation and intellectual independence.

After graduating from University College in 1902, Joyce briefly moved to Paris to study medicine, but he soon abandoned his medical studies to pursue a literary career. The death of his mother in 1903 brought him back to Dublin, where he began writing and teaching to support himself. During this period, he also met Nora Barnacle, a young woman from Galway who would become his lifelong partner and muse. Their relationship was marked by deep affection and mutual support, despite the many challenges they faced.

Joyce's early literary efforts included a collection of short stories, "Dubliners," and a novel, "Stephen Hero," which would later evolve into "A Portrait of the Artist as a Young Man." "Dubliners," published in 1914 after numerous rejections, consists of fifteen stories that portray the lives of ordinary Dubliners with unflinching realism and psychological depth. The collection is notable for its use of epiphanies, moments of sudden revelation or insight experienced by the characters. "The Dead," the final story in the collection, is often considered one of the greatest short stories in the English language.

In "A Portrait of the Artist as a Young Man," published in 1916, Joyce presents a semi-autobiographical account of the early life and artistic development of Stephen Dedalus, a character based on himself. The novel traces Stephen's growth from a sensitive child to a rebellious young artist, exploring themes of identity, religion, and the struggle for artistic freedom. "A Portrait" is celebrated for its innovative use of stream-of-consciousness technique, which allows readers to experience the protagonist's inner thoughts and emotions in a direct and immediate way.

In 1904, Joyce and Nora Barnacle left Ireland to live in continental Europe. They spent the next several years moving between cities such as Trieste, Zurich, and Paris, struggling with financial difficulties and Joyce's health problems. Despite these challenges, Joyce continued to write and develop his unique literary style. During this period, he also worked as a language teacher and translator, further honing his linguistic skills and deepening his appreciation for the nuances of language.

Joyce's next major work, "Ulysses," was published in 1922. The novel, which takes place over the course of a single day, June 16, 1904, in Dublin, follows the experiences of three main characters: Leopold Bloom, a Jewish advertising agent; his wife, Molly Bloom; and Stephen Dedalus, the protagonist from "A Portrait." "Ulysses" is renowned for its complexity, innovative narrative techniques, and rich allusions to classical literature, particularly Homer's "Odyssey."

Each chapter of "Ulysses" employs a different literary style, ranging from stream-of-consciousness and interior monologue to parodies of various literary forms. This diversity of styles reflects Joyce's belief in the boundless potential of language and narrative form. The novel's use of interior monologue, in particular, provides a deep and nuanced portrayal of the characters' inner lives, capturing the complexity and fluidity of human thought.

"Ulysses" faced considerable controversy upon its publication, primarily due to its explicit content and frank depiction of sexuality. The novel was initially serialized in the American journal "The Little Review," but legal action was taken against the publication for obscenity, leading to a ban on the book in the United States and the United Kingdom. Despite these challenges, "Ulysses" gained a devoted readership and critical acclaim, establishing Joyce as a leading figure in modernist literature.

Joyce's final and most enigmatic work, "Finnegans Wake," was published in 1939 after seventeen years of writing and revision. The novel is characterized by its dense and intricate language, which blends multiple languages, puns, and allusions into a complex and often bewildering tapestry of meaning. "Finnegans Wake" eschews conventional narrative structure, instead presenting a cyclical and dreamlike exploration of human history, mythology, and consciousness.

The book's title refers to the Irish ballad "Finnegan's Wake," which tells the story of a builder named Tim Finnegan who is resurrected from the dead during his own wake. This theme of cyclical renewal and transformation is central to the novel, reflecting Joyce's fascination with the eternal recurrence of human experience. "Finnegans Wake" has been both praised for its linguistic inventiveness and criticized for its opacity, but it remains a seminal work in the study of modernist literature.

Joyce's personal life was marked by significant challenges, including his struggles with his eyesight and financial difficulties. He underwent numerous eye surgeries throughout his life, and his deteriorating vision often hindered his writing. Despite these hardships, Joyce remained committed to his literary endeavors, drawing strength from his close relationships with Nora and their children, Giorgio and Lucia.

Lucia Joyce, in particular, faced her own struggles with mental illness, which deeply affected Joyce and his family. Lucia was diagnosed with schizophrenia, and her condition required extensive care and treatment. Joyce's concern for his daughter and his efforts to support her through her illness added another layer of complexity to his personal life and creative work.

Throughout his career, Joyce maintained a deep connection to his Irish heritage and the city of Dublin, despite his physical distance from Ireland. His works are imbued with a rich sense of place, capturing the nuances of Dublin's streets, its social dynamics, and its cultural traditions. This deep engagement with his homeland, combined with his innovative narrative techniques, has made Joyce a central figure in Irish literature and a key influence on subsequent generations of writers.

In addition to his novels, Joyce also wrote poetry and short fiction. His collection of poems, "Chamber Music" (1907), reflects his early lyrical style, while "Pomes Penyeach" (1927) showcases his later, more experimental approach to verse. Joyce's shorter fiction, such as the stories in "Dubliners," demonstrates his keen eye for detail and his ability to capture the intricacies of everyday life.

Joyce's influence on literature is profound and far-reaching. His innovative use of language and narrative form has inspired countless writers and scholars, and his works continue to be studied and celebrated for their complexity and depth. "Ulysses," in particular, is often regarded as one of the greatest novels of the 20th century, and its impact on the development of modernist literature cannot be overstated.

In addition to his literary achievements, Joyce's life and work have also been the subject of extensive critical analysis and biographical study. His correspondence, notebooks, and other personal documents provide valuable insights into his creative process and his intellectual world. Scholars have explored various aspects of Joyce's writing, from his use of myth and symbolism to his engagement with contemporary politics and culture.

James Joyce's legacy extends beyond the realm of literature. His exploration of the human psyche, his innovative narrative techniques, and his deep engagement with the complexities of modern life have made him a towering figure in the history of art and thought. Joyce's works challenge readers to think deeply about the nature of identity, the power of language, and the intricacies of human experience, ensuring that his influence will endure for generations to come.

Joyce passed away on January 13, 1941, in Zurich, Switzerland, following complications from surgery. His death marked the end of a remarkable literary career, but his influence on the world of literature remains undiminished. Joyce's works continue to be read, studied, and celebrated around the world, testifying to the enduring power of his artistic vision and his profound understanding of the human condition.

Chapter 15: Marcel Proust

Marcel Proust, born Valentin Louis Georges Eugène Marcel Proust on July 10, 1871, in Auteuil, France, is renowned as one of the greatest literary figures of the 20th century. His monumental work, "À la recherche du temps perdu" ("In Search of Lost Time"), is celebrated for its deep psychological insight, intricate narrative structure, and profound exploration of memory and time. Proust's life and writing reflect his complex and multifaceted personality, his acute observations of human behavior, and his relentless pursuit of artistic truth.

Proust was born into a well-to-do bourgeois family. His father, Adrien Proust, was a prominent physician and epidemiologist, known for his work on cholera, while his mother, Jeanne Weil Proust, came from a wealthy and cultured Jewish family. Proust was a frail child, suffering from severe asthma and other health issues that would plague him throughout his life. Despite his delicate health, he was an intellectually gifted and precocious child, displaying an early talent for writing and a keen interest in literature.

Proust received his education at the Lycée Condorcet in Paris, where he excelled academically and formed important friendships that would influence his later work. He was particularly close to Jacques Bizet, the son of the composer Georges Bizet, and Lucien Daudet, the son of the writer Alphonse Daudet. These friendships provided Proust with entry into the artistic and literary circles of Paris, where he was exposed to the works of contemporary writers and thinkers.

After completing his baccalauréat in 1889, Proust studied law at the École Libre des Sciences Politiques (now Sciences Po) in Paris. However, his true passion lay in literature, and he soon became involved in the literary and social life of the city. He began frequenting the salons of the Parisian aristocracy, where he encountered many of the figures who would later serve as models for the characters in his novel. Proust's early literary efforts included contributions to the literary journal "Le Banquet" and the publication of his first book, "Les Plaisirs et les Jours" ("Pleasures and Days") in 1896, a collection of short stories, essays, and poems.

Proust's early writing showed his talent for capturing the subtleties of human emotion and social interaction, but it was not until he embarked on the ambitious project of "In Search of Lost Time" that he fully realized his artistic potential. The idea for the novel began to take shape in the early 1900s, influenced by Proust's reading of philosophers such as Henri Bergson, whose ideas on memory and time deeply resonated with him. Proust was also inspired by his own experiences, particularly his relationships with his family, friends, and lovers.

The death of Proust's mother in 1905 was a turning point in his life. Deeply affected by her loss, he withdrew from society and began to focus intensively on his writing. Proust's health continued to deteriorate, and he became increasingly reclusive, often writing through the night and sleeping during the day. He transformed his bedroom into a soundproofed sanctuary, lined with cork to keep out noise, where he could concentrate on his work undisturbed.

"In Search of Lost Time," originally published in seven volumes between 1913 and 1927, is an epic exploration of memory, time, and the nature of human experience. The novel is narrated by an unnamed protagonist, often identified with Proust himself, who reflects on his past and seeks to understand the meaning of his life. The narrative structure of the novel is complex and nonlinear, moving fluidly between different periods of the narrator's life and interweaving multiple themes and motifs.

The first volume, "Du côté de chez Swann" ("Swann's Way"), introduces the central themes and characters of the novel. It opens with the narrator's recollections of his childhood in the fictional town of Combray, based on Proust's own experiences in Illiers. The famous "madeleine episode," in which the taste of a madeleine dipped in tea triggers a flood of involuntary memories, exemplifies Proust's exploration of the ways in which sensory experiences can evoke the past. The second part of "Swann's Way" focuses on the story of Charles Swann, a wealthy and cultured Jewish man who becomes infatuated with Odette de Crécy, a courtesan. Swann's obsessive love for Odette and his subsequent disillusionment serve as a microcosm of the novel's broader themes of desire, memory, and the passage of time.

The subsequent volumes of "In Search of Lost Time" continue to delve into the narrator's experiences and observations of the world around him. "À l'ombre des jeunes filles en fleurs" ("In the Shadow of Young Girls in Flower") depicts the narrator's adolescence and his encounters with various social milieus, including the aristocratic Guermantes family and the artistic circles of Paris. The novel's rich descriptions of society and its intricate portrayal of relationships reveal Proust's keen insight into human nature and the complexities of social interaction.

"Le Côté de Guermantes" ("The Guermantes Way") and "Sodome et Gomorrhe" ("Sodom and Gomorrah") explore the narrator's further integration into high society and his growing awareness of the duplicity and superficiality of the social world. These volumes also address themes of homosexuality and the nature of sexual desire, reflecting Proust's own experiences and observations. The character of Baron de Charlus, a complex and multifaceted figure, serves as a focal point for these explorations, embodying the tensions between public persona and private identity.

"La Prisonnière" ("The Captive") and "Albertine disparue" ("The Fugitive") focus on the narrator's tumultuous relationship with Albertine, a young woman whose elusive and enigmatic nature captivates him. These volumes delve into the themes of jealousy, possession, and the search for understanding in the context of romantic relationships. The narrator's obsessive need to control and possess

Albertine ultimately leads to his profound disillusionment and recognition of the impossibility of truly knowing another person.

The final volume, "Le Temps retrouvé" ("Time Regained"), brings the novel full circle, as the narrator reflects on the meaning of his past and the transformative power of art. He realizes that the act of writing itself offers a means of transcending the limitations of time and mortality, allowing him to capture and preserve the essence of his experiences. The novel's conclusion affirms the redemptive and enduring value of artistic creation, even in the face of the inexorable passage of time.

Throughout "In Search of Lost Time," Proust's prose is characterized by its long, intricate sentences, rich imagery, and profound psychological insight. His writing style, often described as "stream-of-consciousness," seeks to capture the fluid and multifaceted nature of human thought and experience. Proust's ability to render the inner lives of his characters with such depth and precision is one of the hallmarks of his genius, making his work a touchstone for subsequent generations of writers and thinkers.

Proust's literary achievements were recognized during his lifetime, though his work initially faced significant obstacles to publication. The first volume of "In Search of Lost Time" was published by the influential editor and publisher Bernard Grasset after being rejected by several other publishers, including André Gide at the prestigious NRF (Nouvelle Revue Française). However, the novel's subsequent success and critical acclaim led to its recognition as a masterpiece of modern literature.

Proust's health continued to decline in his later years, and he became increasingly isolated, devoting himself entirely to his writing. Despite his physical frailty, he remained intellectually vigorous, meticulously revising and refining his work. He died on November 18, 1922, at the age of 51, leaving behind a literary legacy that would continue to shape the course of literature and thought for generations to come.

In the decades since his death, Proust's influence has only grown, with his work inspiring countless writers, scholars, and readers. His exploration of memory and time, his profound psychological insights, and his innovative narrative techniques have made "In Search of Lost Time" a central text in the study of modern literature. Proust's ability to capture the intricacies of human experience with such depth and precision ensures that his work remains a vital and enduring part of the literary canon.

Proust's legacy extends beyond the realm of literature, influencing fields such as psychology, philosophy, and cultural studies. His exploration of the nature of memory and the self resonates with contemporary understandings of human cognition and identity, while his reflections on art and society continue to inform debates about the role of the artist in the modern world. Proust's work challenges readers to confront the complexities of their own experiences and to find meaning in the fleeting and ephemeral nature of life.

Marcel Proust's life and work exemplify the power of literature to transcend the limitations of time and space, offering readers a window into the profound depths of human experience. His relentless pursuit of artistic truth, his acute observations of the world around him, and his innovative narrative techniques have left an indelible mark on the landscape of modern literature. Proust's exploration of memory, time, and the nature of human experience continues to inspire and challenge readers, ensuring that his legacy will endure for generations to come.

Chapter 16: Maya Angelou

Maya Angelou, born Marguerite Annie Johnson on April 4, 1928, in St. Louis, Missouri, emerged as one of the most influential voices in contemporary literature. Her multifaceted career spanned over six decades, encompassing a myriad of roles including poet, memoirist, novelist, educator, dramatist, producer, actress, historian, filmmaker, and civil rights activist. Her life and work are a testament to her resilience, creativity, and unwavering commitment to social justice.

Angelou's early years were marked by upheaval and trauma. Her parents' tumultuous marriage led to their separation when she was just three years old, after which she and her older brother, Bailey, were sent to live with their grandmother in Stamps, Arkansas. This period of her life, filled with the harsh realities of racial discrimination and the strictures of the Jim Crow South, deeply influenced her later work. The brutal experience of being raped by her mother's boyfriend when she was eight years old had a profound impact on her. The trauma was compounded when she revealed the assault to her family, and her assailant was later found dead, likely at the hands of her uncles. Believing her voice had caused his death, Angelou fell silent and did not speak for almost five years. During this time of selective mutism, she developed a profound love for literature and learned the power of words, even if she did not speak them.

Angelou's teenage years saw her return to her mother's care in San Francisco. She attended the California Labor School and studied dance and drama. At sixteen, she became the first African American female streetcar conductor in San Francisco. Her early adulthood was filled with varied experiences, including a brief stint as a single mother following the birth of her son, Guy. To support herself and her son, she worked as a cook, waitress, and nightclub dancer. Her passion for the arts, however, remained undiminished, and she soon found herself drawn into the world of performance and writing.

Her first major breakthrough came with the publication of her autobiography, "I Know Why the Caged Bird Sings," in 1969. The book, which details her childhood and early adulthood, was groundbreaking for its honest portrayal of the complexities of black womanhood in America. It was an immediate critical and commercial success, earning Angelou widespread acclaim and establishing her as a powerful new voice in American literature. The book's title, taken from a poem by Paul Laurence Dunbar, symbolizes the longing for freedom and equality that characterized much of her work.

"I Know Why the Caged Bird Sings" was the first of seven autobiographies that Angelou would publish over the next few decades. Each of these works provides a rich, nuanced portrait of her life and times. In "Gather Together in My Name" (1974), she recounts her experiences as a young single mother navigating the challenges of work and relationships. "Singin' and Swingin' and Gettin' Merry Like Christmas" (1976) chronicles her early career as a performer and her travels with the European tour of "Porgy and Bess." "The Heart of a Woman" (1981) explores her involvement in the civil rights movement and her relationships with prominent figures like Martin Luther King Jr. and Malcolm X. "All God's Children Need Traveling Shoes" (1986) details her time in Ghana during the 1960s and her exploration of her African heritage. "A Song Flung Up to Heaven" (2002) covers the turbulent years of the late 1960s and her return to the United States following the assassinations of Malcolm X and Martin Luther King Jr. Her final autobiography, "Mom & Me & Mom" (2013), provides a poignant look at her relationship with her mother, Vivian Baxter.

In addition to her autobiographies, Angelou published several volumes of poetry, including "Just Give Me a Cool Drink of Water 'fore I Diiie" (1971), which was nominated for the Pulitzer Prize. Her poetry, like her prose, is marked by its lyricism, emotional depth, and commitment to social justice. Poems such as "Phenomenal Woman," "Still I Rise," and "On the Pulse of Morning," which she recited at

President Bill Clinton's inauguration in 1993, have become iconic expressions of resilience and empowerment.

Angelou's contributions to literature and culture extend beyond her written work. She was a prolific performer and educator, bringing her powerful voice and presence to stages and classrooms around the world. Her work as a civil rights activist included close associations with leaders like Martin Luther King Jr. and Malcolm X, and she was a prominent advocate for equality and justice throughout her life. Her ability to connect with people from all walks of life, combined with her eloquence and insight, made her a sought-after speaker and teacher.

In the realm of performance, Angelou's talents were equally impressive. She appeared in numerous plays, films, and television shows, often bringing her unique perspective and voice to her roles. She received critical acclaim for her performance in the 1977 television adaptation of Alex Haley's "Roots," and her screenplay for the 1972 film "Georgia, Georgia" made her the first African American woman to have a screenplay produced. Her directorial debut, the 1998 film "Down in the Delta," is a poignant exploration of family, identity, and redemption.

Angelou's life was also marked by numerous honors and awards. She received the Presidential Medal of Freedom, the highest civilian honor in the United States, from President Barack Obama in 2010. In addition to numerous honorary degrees and literary awards, she was appointed by President Jimmy Carter to the National Commission on the Observance of International Women's Year and by President Gerald Ford to the American Revolution Bicentennial Advisory Council. Her work and legacy continue to be celebrated and studied by scholars, writers, and activists around the world.

Maya Angelou's legacy is one of profound impact and enduring inspiration. Her ability to transcend the personal and speak to universal human experiences has made her an enduring figure in American culture. Her work, characterized by its honesty, courage, and eloquence, continues to resonate with readers and audiences, offering insights into the complexities of identity, race, and the human spirit. Through her writing, performance, and activism, Angelou has left an indelible mark on the world, reminding us of the power of words and the importance of standing up for justice and equality. Her life story, marked by triumphs and challenges, is a testament to the strength of the human spirit and the transformative power of creativity and resilience.

Chapter 17: Andy Warhol

Andy Warhol, born Andrew Warhola on August 6, 1928, in Pittsburgh, Pennsylvania, is often heralded as a leading figure in the visual art movement known as Pop Art. Warhol's influence on contemporary art and culture extends far beyond his iconic paintings, silkscreens, and films; he redefined what it meant to be an artist in the modern age, blending art with celebrity culture, commercialism, and media.

Warhol's early life was marked by the working-class immigrant experience. His parents, Andrej and Julia Warhola, were Slovakian immigrants who settled in Pittsburgh. His father worked in a coal mine, and his mother took on various odd jobs to help make ends meet. As a child, Warhol was often sick, spending significant time bedridden, which fostered his love for drawing and his fascination with celebrity magazines and comic strips. These interests would later profoundly influence his artistic style and thematic choices.

Warhol's formal art education began at the Carnegie Institute of Technology (now Carnegie Mellon University), where he studied commercial art. He moved to New York City in 1949, beginning a career as a commercial illustrator. His early work, particularly his illustrations for advertisements, record albums, and magazines, showcased his ability to blend fine art with commercial techniques, foreshadowing his later works. His distinct style, characterized by bold lines and an emphasis on branding, began to attract attention in the commercial art world.

The 1960s marked a turning point in Warhol's career as he transitioned from commercial art to fine art. He began experimenting with silkscreen printing, a technique that allowed him to produce multiple copies of a single image, challenging the traditional notions of art as unique, handcrafted objects. This method became a hallmark of his work, exemplified by his iconic Campbell's Soup Cans series in

1962. By elevating mundane consumer goods to the status of high art, Warhol questioned the distinctions between high and low culture and critiqued the burgeoning consumerism of American society.

Warhol's fascination with celebrity culture is evident in his portraits of famous personalities, including Marilyn Monroe, Elvis Presley, and Elizabeth Taylor. His Marilyn Diptych (1962), featuring repeated images of Monroe, explores themes of fame, mortality, and the commodification of identity. By using silkscreen printing to replicate Monroe's image multiple times, Warhol highlighted the mass production of celebrity personas and the fleeting nature of fame. This work, like many others, underscores his interest in the intersection of media, fame, and art.

The Factory, Warhol's New York City studio, became a hub of creativity and experimentation in the 1960s. It attracted a diverse group of artists, musicians, writers, and socialites, fostering a vibrant, collaborative atmosphere that challenged conventional boundaries between art and life. The Factory was notorious for its wild parties and avant-garde happenings, which Warhol often documented through film and photography. This environment was crucial in developing his multimedia approach to art, encompassing painting, sculpture, film, and photography.

Warhol's foray into filmmaking further expanded his influence on contemporary culture. His films, such as "Sleep" (1963), which depicts a man sleeping for five hours, and "Empire" (1964), an eight-hour continuous shot of the Empire State Building, challenged traditional cinematic norms and explored themes of time, voyeurism, and reality. His film "Chelsea Girls" (1966) gained significant attention for its innovative split-screen format and candid portrayal of the lives of New York City bohemians. Warhol's approach to film, characterized by its raw, unfiltered style and focus on everyday life, prefigured many elements of reality television and independent film.

Despite his avant-garde reputation, Warhol achieved significant commercial success during his lifetime. He was one of the first artists to understand and exploit the power of media and celebrity, becoming a celebrity in his own right. His persona—complete with his platinum wig, dark glasses, and enigmatic demeanor—was as carefully constructed as his art. Warhol's self-promotion tactics, including his frequent appearances in the media and his strategic use of his own image, prefigured the celebrity culture that would dominate the late 20th and early 21st centuries.

Warhol's later work continued to explore themes of celebrity, mortality, and consumer culture, but it also took on a darker, more introspective tone. Following a near-fatal shooting by radical feminist Valerie Solanas in 1968, Warhol's work began to reflect a more pronounced awareness of death and vulnerability. His series of "Death and Disaster" paintings, which included images of car crashes, electric chairs, and civil rights protests, starkly contrasted with the bright, playful colors of his earlier works. These pieces underscored his ongoing preoccupation with the darker aspects of modern life and the ways in which the media sensationalizes tragedy.

In the 1980s, Warhol experienced a resurgence in popularity, collaborating with younger artists like Jean-Michel Basquiat, Francesco Clemente, and Keith Haring. These collaborations bridged the gap between different generations of artists and highlighted Warhol's enduring relevance in the art world. His work from this period, characterized by a return to hand-painted images and a renewed focus on religious themes, showcased his ability to adapt and remain innovative.

Warhol's impact on contemporary art and culture is immeasurable. He challenged traditional notions of art, blurring the lines between high and low culture, commercial and fine art, and artist and celebrity. His work anticipated many aspects of today's media-saturated society, from the cult of celebrity to the commodification of identity. Warhol's exploration of consumerism, fame, and media continues to resonate with artists, critics, and audiences, making him a pivotal figure in the history of modern art.

Beyond his artistic contributions, Warhol's legacy includes his influence on the art market and the way artists perceive their role in society. He was one of the first artists to recognize and leverage the commercial potential of his work, establishing a blueprint for future generations of artists. His savvy understanding of branding, self-promotion, and the art market helped to redefine the economics of the art world.

Warhol's philanthropic efforts also left a lasting impact. He established the Andy Warhol Foundation for the Visual Arts in 1987, shortly before his death, to support contemporary art and artists. The foundation has since become one of the most significant grant-making organizations in the art world, continuing Warhol's legacy of fostering creativity and innovation.

Andy Warhol's death on February 22, 1987, marked the end of an era, but his influence endures. His work continues to be exhibited and studied, and his ideas about art, media, and culture remain relevant in today's digital age. Warhol's ability to capture the zeitgeist of his time and anticipate future trends solidifies his place as a visionary artist whose impact extends far beyond the confines of the art world.

Chapter 18: Salvador Dalí

Salvador Dalí, born Salvador Domingo Felipe Jacinto Dalí i Domènech on May 11, 1904, in Figueres, Catalonia, Spain, is one of the most celebrated and controversial figures in the history of modern art. Renowned for his surrealist works, Dalí's artistic output extends far beyond his iconic paintings. He was a multifaceted artist whose oeuvre includes sculptures, films, photography, performance art, and writing, and his influence can be seen across various facets of contemporary culture.

Dalí's early life was marked by an intense and somewhat tumultuous family environment. His father, Salvador Dalí i Cusí, was a strict and authoritarian notary, while his mother, Felipa Domènech Ferrés, encouraged his artistic endeavors. The early death of his older brother, also named Salvador, profoundly impacted Dalí, who believed he was his brother's reincarnation. This belief shaped much of his identity and artistic vision, infusing his work with themes of duality, death, and rebirth.

Dalí's artistic talent was evident from a young age, and he received his formal education at the Royal Academy of Fine Arts of San Fernando in Madrid. However, his rebellious nature and refusal to conform to academic standards led to his expulsion in 1926. Despite this setback, Dalí's time in Madrid was crucial in his development as an artist. He immersed himself in the works of the Old Masters and experimented with various styles, from Impressionism and Cubism to Futurism. It was also during this period that he forged important relationships with other influential figures, including poet Federico García Lorca and filmmaker Luis Buñuel.

Dalí's move to Paris in 1929 marked the beginning of his association with the Surrealist movement. Surrealism, founded by André Breton, sought to unlock the creative potential of the unconscious mind by embracing dreams, fantasies, and irrationality.

Dalí quickly became a prominent member of the group, contributing to its development with his unique vision and techniques. His "paranoiac-critical method," a process he developed to access his subconscious, involved inducing a state of self-induced paranoia to create hallucinatory images. This method allowed him to juxtapose incongruous objects and ideas, resulting in some of his most famous works.

One of Dalí's most iconic paintings, "The Persistence of Memory" (1931), exemplifies his mastery of the surrealist aesthetic. The painting, featuring melting clocks draped over a barren landscape, challenges conventional perceptions of time and reality. The dreamlike quality and meticulous detail of the work encapsulate Dalí's ability to blend hyper-realism with fantastical elements. This piece, like many others, reflects his fascination with the fluidity of time, the unconscious mind, and the exploration of personal and universal themes.

Dalí's relationship with Gala, born Elena Ivanovna Diakonova, was central to both his personal life and artistic career. Gala, who was ten years his senior, became his muse, collaborator, and eventual wife. Their partnership was both passionate and complex, with Gala exerting a profound influence on Dalí's work. She appeared in many of his paintings and was a constant source of inspiration and support. Their unconventional marriage, marked by mutual dependence and creative synergy, was a driving force behind much of Dalí's artistic output.

Throughout the 1930s and 1940s, Dalí's work continued to evolve, incorporating elements of classical art and science. His fascination with nuclear physics, sparked by the discovery of atomic energy, led to what he termed his "Nuclear Mysticism" period. Paintings from this era, such as "The Sacrament of the Last Supper" (1955) and "Galatea of the Spheres" (1952), reflect his interest in the intersection of science, religion, and mysticism. These works, characterized by their meticulous detail and symbolic content, illustrate Dalí's ability to fuse disparate concepts into cohesive and visually stunning compositions.

Dalí's foray into film was another significant aspect of his artistic career. His collaborations with Luis Buñuel resulted in two of the most influential surrealist films: "Un Chien Andalou" (1929) and "L'Age d'Or" (1930). These films, known for their shocking imagery and non-linear narratives, challenged traditional cinematic conventions and explored themes of desire, violence, and the subconscious. Dalí's involvement in film extended beyond his work with Buñuel; he collaborated with Alfred Hitchcock on the dream sequence for "Spellbound" (1945) and worked with Walt Disney on the animated short "Destino" (1945), which was eventually completed in 2003.

Dalí's flamboyant personality and penchant for self-promotion made him a cultural icon. His meticulously groomed mustache, eccentric wardrobe, and theatrical behavior were as much a part of his artistic persona as his works. He understood the power of media and used it to his advantage, cultivating a public image that was both provocative and enigmatic. This self-created mythos extended to his writings, including his autobiography "The Secret Life of Salvador Dalí" (1942), which offers a surreal and highly stylized account of his life and thoughts.

In addition to his contributions to painting and film, Dalí explored various other media, including sculpture, jewelry design, and performance art. His sculptural works, such as "Lobster Telephone" (1936) and "Mae West Lips Sofa" (1937), exemplify his ability to transform everyday objects into surrealist art. These pieces, often infused with humor and eroticism, challenge viewers to reconsider their perceptions of reality and the ordinary. Dalí's jewelry designs, created in collaboration with the New York jeweler Carlos Alemany, are intricate and imaginative, featuring surrealist motifs rendered in precious metals and gemstones.

Dalí's impact on contemporary culture extends far beyond the realm of visual art. His influence can be seen in fashion, advertising, literature, and music. Designers like Elsa Schiaparelli and Jean-Paul

Gaultier drew inspiration from Dalí's surrealist imagery, while his collaboration with Schiaparelli on the "Lobster Dress" (1937) remains an iconic example of the fusion of art and fashion. Dalí's work also inspired musicians, including the rock band Pink Floyd, who used his imagery in their album art, and artists like David Bowie, who incorporated surrealist elements into their performances and personas.

Despite his immense success and popularity, Dalí's later years were not without controversy. His support for Francisco Franco's fascist regime in Spain and his contentious relationship with fellow surrealists, including André Breton, led to his expulsion from the Surrealist movement in 1939. Breton famously anagrammatized Dalí's name to "Avida Dollars," criticizing his commercialism and perceived betrayal of surrealist ideals. Dalí, however, remained unapologetic, embracing his role as a provocateur and continuing to push the boundaries of art and creativity.

In the 1970s and 1980s, Dalí's health began to decline, exacerbated by the death of Gala in 1982. He became increasingly reclusive, spending his final years in his castle in Púbol, Catalonia. Despite his declining health, he continued to work, producing drawings, prints, and sculptures. His last major project, the Dalí Theatre-Museum in Figueres, opened in 1974 and stands as a testament to his lifelong dedication to art. The museum, designed by Dalí himself, houses a vast collection of his works and remains one of the most visited art museums in Spain.

Salvador Dalí died on January 23, 1989, in Figueres, leaving behind a legacy that continues to captivate and inspire. His contributions to art, culture, and the exploration of the human psyche are immeasurable. Dalí's ability to blend reality with fantasy, to challenge perceptions and provoke thought, has cemented his place as one of the most influential and enigmatic artists of the 20th century. His work invites viewers to question the nature of reality and the power of the imagination, making him a true master of surrealism and a visionary whose impact will endure for generations to come.

Dalí's life and work exemplify the power of creativity to transcend conventional boundaries and explore the depths of the human experience. His unique vision, relentless innovation, and ability to fuse disparate elements into cohesive and compelling works of art have left an indelible mark on the world of art and beyond. Through his paintings, films, sculptures, and writings, Dalí invites us to look beyond the surface and explore the surreal and the sublime, reminding us of the limitless potential of the imagination.

Chapter 19: Coco Chanel

Coco Chanel, born Gabrielle Bonheur Chanel on August 19, 1883, in Saumur, France, is one of the most influential figures in the history of fashion. Chanel revolutionized women's fashion by introducing designs that emphasized comfort, simplicity, and elegance. Her impact on the fashion industry extends far beyond her iconic creations; she redefined modern femininity and left an enduring legacy that continues to influence contemporary fashion.

Chanel's early life was marked by hardship and adversity. Her mother, Jeanne Devolle, died when Gabrielle was just 12 years old, and her father, Albert Chanel, abandoned her and her siblings shortly thereafter. Chanel and her sisters were sent to the convent of Aubazine in central France, where they were raised by nuns. The strict, austere environment of the convent left a lasting impression on Chanel, influencing her later design philosophy with its emphasis on simplicity and functional beauty. The nuns taught her to sew, a skill that would become the foundation of her career.

After leaving the convent, Chanel sought to forge her path. She worked as a seamstress and a cabaret singer, adopting the nickname "Coco" during this period. The origins of the nickname are uncertain; some suggest it was derived from a popular song she sang, while others believe it was a term of endearment given to her by admirers. Despite her ambitions, Chanel struggled to make a name for herself until she met Étienne Balsan, a wealthy textile heir, who became her lover and benefactor. Balsan introduced her to the world of high society and provided her with the financial support to open her first shop in 1910.

Chanel's first venture was a millinery shop on Rue Cambon in Paris, where she began designing and selling hats. Her designs quickly gained popularity among the elite, and by 1913, she had expanded her business to Deauville, a fashionable seaside resort. It was in Deauville that Chanel introduced her first line of clothing, which included simple jersey dresses and relaxed, sporty pieces inspired by menswear. Her designs were a radical departure from the corseted, ornate fashions of the time, emphasizing comfort and ease of movement. This approach resonated with modern women seeking freedom from the constraints of traditional fashion.

World War I played a significant role in the evolution of Chanel's designs. The war necessitated practical clothing for women who were entering the workforce and taking on roles traditionally held by men. Chanel's use of jersey, a fabric previously reserved for men's underwear, was revolutionary. It was inexpensive, comfortable, and draped well, making it ideal for the relaxed silhouettes she favored. Her designs, including the iconic sailor blouse and the little black dress, became synonymous with modern, independent women. The little black dress, introduced in 1926, was particularly significant; it transformed the color black from a symbol of mourning into a chic, versatile staple of every woman's wardrobe.

Chanel's success continued to grow throughout the 1920s and 1930s. She expanded her brand to include perfumes, jewelry, and accessories, each embodying her signature style of understated elegance. In 1921, she introduced Chanel No. 5, a fragrance that would become one of the most famous and enduring perfumes in history. Unlike traditional floral scents, Chanel No. 5 was a complex blend of aldehydes and synthetic compounds, creating a unique, modern fragrance. The perfume's minimalist bottle design, with its clean lines and simple label, reflected Chanel's aesthetic of refined simplicity.

Chanel's romantic relationships also influenced her career. Her affair with Arthur "Boy" Capel, a wealthy English polo player, provided both financial backing and emotional support. Capel's tragic death in a car accident in 1919 deeply affected Chanel, and she later referred to him as the love of her life. Her relationship with the Duke of Westminster, one of the richest men in the world, introduced her to British aristocracy and inspired her use of tweeds and plaids in her designs. These relationships, along with her friendships with influential artists and intellectuals, including Pablo Picasso, Igor Stravinsky, and Jean Cocteau, enriched her creative vision and expanded her social network.

Despite her success, Chanel's life was not without controversy. During World War II, she closed her fashion house and retreated to the Hôtel Ritz in Paris, where she lived during the German occupation. Her relationship with a Nazi officer, Hans Günther von Dincklage, led to accusations of collaboration and tarnished her reputation. After the war, Chanel faced criticism and ostracism, prompting her to leave Paris and live in Switzerland for several years.

Chanel's comeback in the fashion world is a testament to her resilience and enduring influence. At the age of 71, she returned to Paris and reopened her fashion house in 1954. Her new collection, though initially met with skepticism, eventually won over critics and clients. Her timeless designs, including the iconic Chanel suit with its boxy jacket and knee-length skirt, became symbols of sophistication and elegance. The suit's tweed fabric, braid trim, and gold buttons have remained enduring elements of the Chanel brand.

Chanel's design philosophy was characterized by a few key principles: simplicity, comfort, and elegance. She believed that fashion should reflect the needs and desires of modern women, allowing them to move freely and express their individuality. Her designs were marked by clean lines, neutral colors, and luxurious fabrics, creating a sophisticated, timeless look. Chanel's influence extended to accessories as well, including her signature quilted handbag, which featured a chain strap that allowed women to carry it on their shoulder, leaving their hands free. This practical yet stylish design became a classic and remains one of the most sought-after luxury handbags.

Chanel's legacy is also evident in her impact on the fashion industry as a whole. She pioneered the concept of the fashion designer as a brand, using her name and image to promote her products. Her business acumen and understanding of marketing and branding helped to establish the modern fashion industry. She was one of the first designers to create a cohesive brand identity, encompassing clothing, accessories, fragrances, and even interior design.

In addition to her contributions to fashion, Chanel's influence extended to broader cultural and social changes. She challenged traditional gender roles and norms, advocating for women's independence and self-expression. Her designs empowered women to dress for themselves rather than for the approval of men. By incorporating elements of menswear into her collections and promoting a more androgynous aesthetic, Chanel helped to redefine femininity and expand the possibilities for women's fashion.

Coco Chanel's death on January 10, 1971, marked the end of an era, but her legacy continues to thrive. The House of Chanel, under the creative direction of designers like Karl Lagerfeld and Virginie Viard, has remained at the forefront of fashion, consistently adapting and evolving while staying true to Chanel's vision. Her timeless designs, innovative spirit, and commitment to elegance have left an indelible mark on the fashion world.

Chapter 20: Steve Jobs

Steve Jobs, born Steven Paul Jobs on February 24, 1955, in San Francisco, California, is one of the most influential figures in the technology industry and modern business. Known for his role as the co-founder, chairman, and CEO of Apple Inc., Jobs' visionary leadership and innovative spirit transformed multiple industries, including personal computing, animated films, music, phones, tablet computing, and digital publishing. His impact on technology and culture is profound, and his legacy continues to shape the way we live and work.

Jobs was born to Joanne Schieble and Abdulfattah Jandali, but he was adopted by Paul and Clara Jobs shortly after his birth. The Jobs family moved to Mountain View, California, in 1961, which would later become the heart of Silicon Valley. Growing up in this environment, Jobs was exposed to the burgeoning technology scene, which ignited his interest in electronics and computing. He attended Homestead High School, where he met Steve Wozniak, a fellow electronics enthusiast who would become his future business partner.

After graduating from high school in 1972, Jobs enrolled at Reed College in Portland, Oregon, but he dropped out after one semester. Despite leaving formal education, he continued to audit classes that interested him, such as calligraphy, which later influenced the typography and design aesthetics of Apple products. Jobs' unconventional educational path reflects his lifelong commitment to following his passions and thinking differently.

In 1974, Jobs returned to California and joined Atari, a pioneering video game company, as a technician. His stint at Atari was brief, but it allowed him to save enough money to embark on a spiritual journey to India in search of enlightenment. This journey had a profound impact on Jobs' philosophy and worldview, influencing his minimalist aesthetic and emphasis on simplicity in design. Upon his return to the

United States, Jobs reconnected with Wozniak, who had been working on a hobbyist computer project.

In 1976, Jobs and Wozniak founded Apple Computer, Inc. in the Jobs family garage, along with Ronald Wayne, who soon left the company. Their first product, the Apple I, was a single-board computer kit that Wozniak designed and Jobs marketed. The Apple I laid the foundation for their next product, the Apple II, which was released in 1977. The Apple II was a groundbreaking success, featuring an integrated keyboard, color graphics, and a built-in programming language. It became one of the first highly successful mass-produced personal computers, propelling Apple into the spotlight and making Jobs and Wozniak wealthy.

The success of the Apple II allowed Jobs to focus on developing more advanced products. In 1980, Apple went public, and Jobs became a multimillionaire. However, the company's next major project, the Apple Lisa, was not as successful. Despite its advanced features, including a graphical user interface (GUI) and a mouse, the Lisa was too expensive for most consumers. Jobs' insistence on perfection and his demanding management style led to tensions within the company, and he was eventually removed from the Lisa project.

Undeterred, Jobs turned his attention to another project within Apple: the Macintosh. Launched in 1984, the Macintosh was the first commercially successful personal computer to feature a GUI and a mouse, making it more user-friendly than previous computers. The iconic "1984" Super Bowl commercial, directed by Ridley Scott, introduced the Macintosh to the world and solidified Jobs' reputation as a marketing genius. Despite its initial success, the Macintosh struggled to gain significant market share, leading to internal conflicts within Apple.

In 1985, following a power struggle with then-CEO John Sculley, Jobs resigned from Apple. His departure marked a turning point in his career. He founded NeXT Inc., a computer platform development company aimed at the higher education and business markets. Although NeXT computers were technologically advanced and featured innovations such as the NeXTSTEP operating system, they were too expensive to achieve widespread adoption. However, NeXT's software and development environment would later play a crucial role in the evolution of Apple's operating systems.

During this period, Jobs also acquired The Graphics Group, later renamed Pixar Animation Studios, from Lucasfilm in 1986. Under Jobs' leadership, Pixar transitioned from a struggling computer hardware company to a groundbreaking animation studio. In 1995, Pixar released "Toy Story," the first feature-length film entirely created with computer-generated imagery (CGI). "Toy Story" was a critical and commercial success, revolutionizing the animation industry and establishing Pixar as a leading studio. Jobs' investment in and management of Pixar highlighted his ability to recognize and nurture innovative potential outside the realm of computing.

In 1996, Apple acquired NeXT for $429 million, bringing Jobs back to the company he co-founded. Initially serving as an advisor, he quickly regained control and was named interim CEO in 1997. Jobs embarked on a mission to revitalize Apple, which was on the brink of bankruptcy. His first major decision was to streamline Apple's product line, eliminating underperforming products and focusing on a few key areas. This strategy, combined with a series of bold marketing campaigns, began to restore Apple's reputation and financial stability.

One of Jobs' most significant achievements during this period was the introduction of the iMac in 1998. Designed by Jony Ive, the iMac featured a striking all-in-one design, colorful translucent casing, and user-friendly setup. The iMac was a commercial success, reinvigorating Apple's brand and proving that consumers valued design and aesthetics as much as functionality. This emphasis on design and user experience became a hallmark of Apple's products under Jobs' leadership.

Jobs' next major breakthrough came with the introduction of the iPod in 2001. The iPod revolutionized the music industry by offering a portable, easy-to-use device capable of storing thousands of songs. The accompanying iTunes software and iTunes Store allowed users to purchase and organize their music digitally, transforming the way people consumed music. The iPod's success helped Apple transition from a computer company to a consumer electronics powerhouse.

In 2007, Jobs unveiled the iPhone, a revolutionary smartphone that combined a phone, an iPod, and an internet communication device into one. The iPhone's multi-touch interface, sleek design, and app ecosystem set a new standard for mobile phones. It quickly became a cultural phenomenon and solidified Apple's dominance in the smartphone market. The introduction of the App Store in 2008 further expanded the iPhone's capabilities, creating a vibrant ecosystem of third-party applications and services.

Jobs' relentless pursuit of innovation continued with the release of the iPad in 2010. The iPad, a tablet computer with a touch interface, created a new category of mobile devices and changed the way people consumed media, accessed information, and performed various tasks. Its success demonstrated Jobs' ability to anticipate and shape consumer trends, further cementing his legacy as a visionary leader.

Throughout his career, Jobs was known for his intense focus on design, quality, and user experience. He believed that technology should be intuitive and accessible, and he pushed his teams to create products that were both functional and beautiful. His attention to detail and insistence on perfection often led to demanding work environments, but it also resulted in groundbreaking products that redefined industries.

Jobs' management style was characterized by a combination of inspiration and intimidation. He was known for his "reality distortion field," a term coined by his colleagues to describe his ability to persuade and motivate others to achieve the seemingly impossible. While his demanding nature could be polarizing, it also fostered a culture of excellence and innovation at Apple. Jobs' charisma and showmanship were evident in his keynote presentations, where he unveiled new products with dramatic flair and captivated audiences with his vision of the future.

Despite his professional success, Jobs faced significant personal challenges. He was diagnosed with a rare form of pancreatic cancer in 2003 and underwent surgery to remove the tumor. He continued to work during his treatment, but his health struggles eventually led him to take multiple medical leaves of absence. In August 2011, Jobs resigned as CEO of Apple, handing over the reins to Tim Cook, his trusted lieutenant. Jobs remained involved with the company as chairman of the board until his death on October 5, 2011.

Steve Jobs' legacy extends far beyond his contributions to Apple and the technology industry. His vision and innovation transformed the way we live, work, and communicate. Jobs' emphasis on design and user experience influenced countless products and industries, from personal computing and mobile devices to music, film, and digital publishing. His ability to anticipate consumer needs and create products that seamlessly integrated into people's lives set a new standard for technology and design.

In addition to his technological innovations, Jobs' impact on business and entrepreneurship is profound. He demonstrated the power of a clear vision, relentless focus, and willingness to take risks. Jobs' approach to leadership and product development has been studied and emulated by entrepreneurs and business leaders around the world. His belief in the importance of passion, perseverance, and thinking differently continues to inspire future generations.

Jobs' story is also a testament to the importance of resilience and adaptability. Despite facing numerous setbacks, including his ouster from Apple and his battle with cancer, he remained committed to his vision and continued to push the boundaries of innovation. His ability to learn from failures and reinvent himself was a key factor in his success.

Steve Jobs' influence on popular culture is equally significant. He became a cultural icon, symbolizing innovation, creativity, and the spirit of Silicon Valley. His life and work have been the subject of numerous books, films, and documentaries, further cementing his status as a visionary leader and shaping the narrative of the digital age.

Chapter 21: Bill Gates

Bill Gates, born William Henry Gates III on October 28, 1955, in Seattle, Washington, is one of the most prominent and influential figures in the world of technology and philanthropy. As the co-founder of Microsoft Corporation, Gates played a crucial role in revolutionizing personal computing, and his work has had a profound impact on modern society. Beyond his contributions to the tech industry, Gates has dedicated a significant portion of his life to philanthropic efforts, making him one of the most renowned philanthropists in history.

Gates was born into an upper-middle-class family; his father, William H. Gates Sr., was a prominent lawyer, and his mother, Mary Maxwell Gates, was a schoolteacher and later a board member of several prominent organizations. Gates' early interest in computing began at the Lakeside School, a private preparatory school in Seattle. It was here that he was introduced to a computer terminal, and he quickly became fascinated with programming. Gates' passion for technology was evident as he spent countless hours writing and debugging code, even creating a computerized version of tic-tac-toe.

In 1973, Gates enrolled at Harvard University, where he pursued a pre-law major but spent much of his time in the computer lab. It was at Harvard that he met Steve Ballmer, who would later become the CEO of Microsoft. Gates' academic performance was exemplary, but his true calling was in computing. In 1975, he dropped out of Harvard to co-found Microsoft with his childhood friend, Paul Allen. Their vision was to create software for the emerging personal computer market.

Microsoft's first major breakthrough came with the development of a version of the BASIC programming language for the Altair 8800, an early personal computer. This success laid the foundation for the company's growth, and Gates and Allen relocated to Albuquerque,

New Mexico, where the Altair manufacturer, MITS, was located. Microsoft soon began to dominate the market for computer languages, and Gates' leadership and strategic acumen were instrumental in this success.

In 1980, IBM approached Microsoft to develop an operating system for its first personal computer. Microsoft did not have an operating system at the time, but Gates saw an opportunity and quickly acquired a system called QDOS (Quick and Dirty Operating System) from a small company named Seattle Computer Products. Microsoft modified and licensed it to IBM as PC-DOS, while retaining the rights to sell it as MS-DOS to other computer manufacturers. This decision proved to be pivotal, as MS-DOS became the standard operating system for the burgeoning personal computer industry.

The success of MS-DOS established Microsoft as a key player in the tech industry, and Gates' leadership propelled the company to new heights. He was known for his relentless work ethic, often working long hours and setting high standards for his employees. Gates' deep technical knowledge and strategic vision enabled him to anticipate industry trends and position Microsoft to capitalize on emerging opportunities. His competitive nature and business acumen were evident in his negotiation tactics and his ability to forge strategic partnerships.

In 1985, Microsoft launched Windows, a graphical operating system that provided a user-friendly interface for PCs. Windows' success was not immediate, but subsequent versions, particularly Windows 3.0 and Windows 95, revolutionized personal computing and solidified Microsoft's dominance in the operating system market. Windows' intuitive interface and wide range of applications made computers accessible to a broader audience, driving the proliferation of personal computers in homes and businesses worldwide.

Gates' leadership style was characterized by his hands-on approach and attention to detail. He was deeply involved in the development of

Microsoft's products, regularly reviewing code and providing feedback to his engineers. Gates' commitment to excellence and innovation fostered a culture of continuous improvement at Microsoft, driving the company to develop groundbreaking software and maintain its competitive edge.

Microsoft's success extended beyond operating systems. The company diversified its product portfolio with the introduction of productivity software like Microsoft Office, which included applications such as Word, Excel, and PowerPoint. Microsoft Office became the standard suite for business productivity, further entrenching Microsoft's position in the software market. Gates' ability to identify and capitalize on market opportunities enabled Microsoft to expand its influence and generate substantial revenue.

Despite his success, Gates faced significant challenges and controversies. In the 1990s, Microsoft became the target of antitrust investigations by the U.S. Department of Justice and the European Commission. The company was accused of engaging in monopolistic practices, such as bundling its Internet Explorer browser with Windows to stifle competition. The legal battles were intense and lengthy, resulting in a settlement that imposed restrictions on Microsoft's business practices. Gates' response to these challenges demonstrated his resilience and strategic thinking, as he navigated the company through regulatory scrutiny while continuing to drive innovation.

In 2000, Gates transitioned from his role as CEO of Microsoft to focus on his philanthropic endeavors. He and his wife, Melinda, established the Bill & Melinda Gates Foundation, which quickly became one of the world's largest and most influential philanthropic organizations. The foundation's mission is to enhance healthcare, reduce extreme poverty, and expand educational opportunities globally. Gates' philanthropic efforts have had a transformative impact on numerous global health initiatives, including efforts to eradicate diseases such as polio and malaria, improve sanitation and hygiene, and support agricultural development in impoverished regions.

One of the foundation's most significant contributions has been its support for global vaccination programs. Gates' commitment to immunization has saved millions of lives and reduced the prevalence of deadly diseases. The foundation's investments in research and development have accelerated the development of new vaccines and treatments, benefiting populations in low-income countries. Gates' focus on data-driven approaches and evidence-based interventions has set a new standard for effective philanthropy.

In addition to global health, the Bill & Melinda Gates Foundation has prioritized education reform in the United States. Gates has been a vocal advocate for improving K-12 education, promoting initiatives such as teacher effectiveness, curriculum development, and technology integration in classrooms. The foundation's grants and partnerships have supported innovative educational programs and research aimed at addressing disparities in educational outcomes and ensuring that all students have access to high-quality education.

Gates' transition from a tech industry titan to a global philanthropist reflects his evolving vision and commitment to making a positive impact on the world. His ability to leverage his wealth, influence, and strategic thinking to address some of the most pressing challenges facing humanity has earned him widespread recognition and respect. Gates' approach to philanthropy is characterized by his focus on measurable results, collaboration with other organizations and governments, and a willingness to take risks to achieve meaningful change.

Despite his philanthropic success, Gates' personal life has faced public scrutiny. In 2021, Gates and Melinda announced their divorce after 27 years of marriage. The dissolution of their marriage raised questions about the future of the foundation, but both Gates and

Melinda have pledged to continue their philanthropic work and maintain their commitment to the foundation's mission.

Gates' legacy is multifaceted, encompassing his contributions to technology, business, and philanthropy. As a tech pioneer, he revolutionized personal computing and transformed Microsoft into one of the world's most valuable companies. His vision and leadership drove the development of software that has become integral to daily life, shaping the way people work, communicate, and access information. Gates' impact on the tech industry is immeasurable, and his innovations continue to influence the evolution of technology.

As a philanthropist, Gates has demonstrated the power of leveraging wealth and influence for the greater good. His strategic approach to philanthropy, focus on data and evidence, and commitment to addressing global health and education challenges have set a new standard for effective giving. Gates' philanthropic efforts have saved lives, improved health outcomes, and expanded educational opportunities for millions of people worldwide.

In addition to his professional and philanthropic achievements, Gates is known for his intellectual curiosity and passion for learning. He is an avid reader and has recommended numerous books on a wide range of topics, from science and technology to history and economics. Gates' dedication to continuous learning and intellectual growth reflects his belief in the importance of knowledge and innovation in solving complex problems.

Gates' influence extends to his role as a thought leader and advocate for addressing global challenges. He has used his platform to raise awareness about issues such as climate change, renewable energy, and sustainable development. Gates' investments in clean energy technologies and his advocacy for policies that promote environmental sustainability underscore his commitment to creating a better future for the planet.

Chapter 22: Mark Zuckerberg

Mark Zuckerberg, born on May 14, 1984, in White Plains, New York, is a prominent figure in the tech industry, best known as the co-founder and CEO of Facebook, Inc., which later rebranded to Meta Platforms, Inc. His journey from a college student to one of the most influential tech entrepreneurs in the world is a testament to his vision, drive, and the transformative power of social media. Zuckerberg's impact on global communication, technology, and business is profound, and his story is one of innovation, controversy, and immense influence.

Zuckerberg grew up in a well-educated and supportive family. His father, Edward Zuckerberg, was a dentist, and his mother, Karen Kempner, was a psychiatrist. Mark showed an early interest in computers and programming. At the age of 12, he created a messaging program called "ZuckNet" that allowed his family's computers to communicate with each other, demonstrating his budding skills and innovative thinking.

He attended Phillips Exeter Academy, an exclusive preparatory school, where he excelled in classical studies and won prizes in science and math. During high school, he built a music player called Synapse Media Player, which used artificial intelligence to learn users' listening habits. Microsoft and AOL expressed interest in buying Synapse and hiring Zuckerberg, but he chose to attend Harvard University instead.

At Harvard, Zuckerberg quickly gained a reputation as a programming prodigy. In his sophomore year, he developed a program called CourseMatch, which helped students select their classes based on the choices of other users. He also created Facemash, a website that allowed users to rate the attractiveness of their fellow students. Facemash was shut down by the university administration due to privacy concerns, but it demonstrated Zuckerberg's interest in creating social networking platforms.

In January 2004, Zuckerberg began working on a new website with his roommates Andrew McCollum, Eduardo Saverin, Chris Hughes, and Dustin Moskovitz. Initially called "The Facebook," the site was launched in February 2004. It was initially limited to Harvard students but quickly expanded to other Ivy League universities and then to colleges and universities across the United States. The site's popularity grew rapidly, and by the end of 2004, it had over one million registered users.

The success of Facebook attracted the attention of investors. In June 2004, Zuckerberg and his co-founders moved to Palo Alto, California, and secured their first investment from PayPal co-founder Peter Thiel. This investment allowed Facebook to expand its infrastructure and hire more staff. Zuckerberg's vision for Facebook was to create a platform that would connect people and allow them to share information easily. He was determined to grow the company rapidly and fend off potential competitors.

One of Zuckerberg's key strengths was his ability to adapt and innovate. He constantly pushed his team to improve the platform and introduce new features. In 2006, Facebook opened its registration to anyone over the age of 13 with a valid email address, which significantly expanded its user base. The introduction of the News Feed feature in 2006 revolutionized the way users interacted with the platform by providing a continuous update of their friends' activities. Despite initial backlash, the News Feed became a central feature of Facebook.

Under Zuckerberg's leadership, Facebook continued to grow exponentially. By 2008, it had surpassed MySpace as the most popular social networking site. The company's success attracted significant investments, including a $240 million investment from Microsoft in 2007, which valued Facebook at $15 billion. Zuckerberg's strategy of prioritizing user growth over immediate profitability paid off, as Facebook became a dominant force in the social media landscape.

Zuckerberg's leadership style has been characterized by his intense focus, resilience, and willingness to take risks. He is known for his hands-on approach and his insistence on maintaining control over the company's strategic direction. Despite his young age, Zuckerberg demonstrated remarkable business acumen and a deep understanding of technology. His ability to anticipate and respond to industry trends allowed Facebook to stay ahead of its competitors.

One of Zuckerberg's most significant achievements was the successful initial public offering (IPO) of Facebook in May 2012. The IPO raised $16 billion, making it one of the largest in tech history. While the IPO faced some initial challenges, it solidified Facebook's position as a major player in the tech industry and provided the company with the financial resources to pursue further growth and innovation.

Zuckerberg's vision for Facebook extended beyond social networking. He sought to create a comprehensive platform that integrated various aspects of people's lives. This vision led to the acquisition of several companies, including Instagram in 2012, WhatsApp in 2014, and Oculus VR in 2014. These acquisitions expanded Facebook's reach and capabilities, allowing it to dominate the social media, messaging, and virtual reality markets. Zuckerberg's strategic acquisitions were instrumental in maintaining Facebook's competitive edge and diversifying its product offerings.

Despite his professional success, Zuckerberg has faced significant challenges and controversies. Facebook has been criticized for its handling of user data, privacy issues, and the spread of misinformation. The Cambridge Analytica scandal in 2018, where it was revealed that the data of millions of Facebook users had been harvested without their consent for political advertising, was a major blow to the company's reputation. Zuckerberg testified before the U.S. Congress to address these concerns and promised to implement changes to protect user data and improve transparency.

The spread of misinformation and hate speech on the platform has been another major issue. Facebook has been criticized for not doing enough to prevent the dissemination of false information and for allowing harmful content to spread. In response, Zuckerberg has committed to investing in artificial intelligence and human moderators to detect and remove inappropriate content. He has also worked on improving the platform's algorithms to prioritize credible information and reduce the visibility of false or misleading content.

In addition to his work with Facebook, Zuckerberg is also known for his philanthropic efforts. In 2010, he signed the Giving Pledge, committing to donate the majority of his wealth to charitable causes. In 2015, Zuckerberg and his wife, Priscilla Chan, announced the creation of the Chan Zuckerberg Initiative (CZI), a philanthropic organization aimed at advancing human potential and promoting equality. The CZI focuses on areas such as education, healthcare, scientific research, and criminal justice reform. Zuckerberg's commitment to philanthropy reflects his desire to use his wealth and influence to make a positive impact on the world.

Education has been a major focus of Zuckerberg's philanthropic efforts. The CZI has invested in initiatives to improve education outcomes, particularly for underserved communities. The organization has supported the development of personalized learning technologies, funded educational research, and provided grants to schools and educational organizations. Zuckerberg's vision for education is to create a more equitable and effective system that empowers all students to succeed.

Healthcare is another key area of focus for the CZI. Zuckerberg and Chan have committed significant resources to biomedical research and the development of new technologies to treat and prevent diseases. The organization has funded initiatives such as the Biohub, a research center that brings together scientists and engineers to collaborate on innovative healthcare solutions. The CZI's investments in healthcare reflect Zuckerberg's belief in the power of science and technology to improve human health and well-being.

Zuckerberg's influence extends beyond his work with Facebook and philanthropy. He has become a prominent voice on issues such as internet regulation, data privacy, and the future of technology. He has called for clearer regulations around data use and privacy and has advocated for policies that promote innovation while protecting users' rights. Zuckerberg's involvement in these discussions highlights his commitment to shaping the future of technology in a responsible and ethical manner.

In recent years, Zuckerberg has focused on the development of the metaverse, a virtual reality space where users can interact with a computer-generated environment and other users. In 2021, Facebook rebranded to Meta Platforms, Inc., reflecting the company's shift towards building the metaverse. Zuckerberg envisions the metaverse as the next evolution of the internet, where people can work, play, and connect in immersive digital environments. This ambitious vision underscores Zuckerberg's commitment to pushing the boundaries of technology and creating new ways for people to connect and interact.

Zuckerberg's journey from a college student to a tech mogul and philanthropist is a remarkable story of innovation, resilience, and impact. His ability to envision the potential of social media and his relentless pursuit of that vision have transformed the way people communicate and connect. Despite the challenges and controversies he has faced, Zuckerberg's influence on the tech industry and global society is undeniable.

His leadership and vision have not only shaped Facebook but have also set the standard for social media platforms worldwide. Zuckerberg's commitment to innovation and his willingness to take risks have driven Facebook's success and enabled the company to remain at the forefront of the tech industry. His focus on user experience, continuous improvement, and strategic growth has established Facebook as a dominant force in the digital age.

Zuckerberg's philanthropic efforts through the Chan Zuckerberg Initiative demonstrate his dedication to using his wealth and influence to address some of the world's most pressing challenges. His investments in education, healthcare, and scientific research reflect his belief in the power of technology and innovation to create a better future. Through his philanthropy, Zuckerberg aims to promote equality and improve the quality of life for people around the world.

As Zuckerberg continues to lead Meta Platforms and pursue his vision for the metaverse, his influence on the future of technology and society remains significant. His commitment to innovation, ethical responsibility, and philanthropy will continue to shape the digital landscape and inspire future generations of tech entrepreneurs and leaders.

Chapter 23: Elon Musk

Elon Musk is a name synonymous with innovation and ambition, often hailed as one of the most influential and creative minds of the 21st century. Born on June 28, 1971, in Pretoria, South Africa, Musk displayed an early aptitude for technology and entrepreneurship. His journey from a curious child to a tech mogul began with his fascination for computers and programming. At the age of 12, he developed and sold a video game called Blastar, showcasing his early talent for software engineering. This initial success hinted at the vast potential that Musk would later realize on a much grander scale.

Musk's educational journey took him to Canada and the United States, where he attended Queen's University before transferring to the University of Pennsylvania. There, he earned dual degrees in physics and economics, laying a strong foundation for his future ventures. His time at Penn was marked by intense intellectual curiosity and a drive to understand the fundamental principles governing the world. This blend of technical knowledge and business acumen would become a hallmark of his career, enabling him to tackle some of the most complex challenges of our time.

After a brief stint at Stanford University, which he left after just two days to pursue entrepreneurial ventures, Musk co-founded Zip2, a company that provided online business directories and maps for newspapers. This venture was his first major success, culminating in a $307 million acquisition by Compaq in 1999. Flush with capital and experience, Musk then turned his attention to financial services, co-founding X.com, an online payment company. X.com eventually became PayPal, a pioneering platform in digital payments. In 2002, PayPal was acquired by eBay for $1.5 billion in stock, cementing Musk's status as a leading figure in the tech industry.

Musk's vision extends far beyond conventional business. He is driven by a desire to address some of humanity's most pressing issues, such as sustainable energy and space exploration. In 2002, he founded SpaceX with the goal of reducing space transportation costs to enable the colonization of Mars. SpaceX faced numerous challenges in its early years, including multiple failed launches. However, Musk's relentless pursuit of innovation paid off when SpaceX became the first privately funded company to send a spacecraft to the International Space Station in 2012. The company's achievements include the development of the Falcon and Starship rockets, both designed for reusable space travel, which could revolutionize the economics of space exploration.

Parallel to his work at SpaceX, Musk became the CEO and product architect of Tesla, Inc., an electric vehicle manufacturer, in 2008. Under his leadership, Tesla has transformed the automotive industry by popularizing electric cars and proving their viability as a sustainable alternative to fossil fuel-powered vehicles. Tesla's Model S, Model 3, Model X, and Model Y have garnered acclaim for their performance, safety, and innovative features. Musk's commitment to advancing battery technology and expanding the global network of Supercharger stations has been crucial in addressing the infrastructure challenges associated with electric vehicles.

In addition to SpaceX and Tesla, Musk has founded or co-founded several other ventures aimed at solving critical global issues. SolarCity, a solar energy services company, was established to promote the adoption of renewable energy sources. OpenAI, a research organization dedicated to ensuring that artificial general intelligence benefits humanity, reflects Musk's concern about the potential risks and ethical implications of advanced AI. The Boring Company, which aims to reduce traffic congestion through the construction of underground transportation tunnels, exemplifies his innovative approach to urban mobility.

One of Musk's most ambitious projects is Neuralink, a neurotechnology company focused on developing brain-computer interface technology. Neuralink's goal is to merge the human brain with artificial intelligence, potentially offering treatments for neurological conditions and enhancing human cognitive abilities. This venture epitomizes Musk's futuristic vision and willingness to explore uncharted territories in science and technology.

Musk's ventures are characterized by a unique combination of audacity, technical prowess, and an unwavering commitment to long-term goals. His approach often involves setting seemingly impossible targets and working tirelessly to achieve them, a strategy that has earned him both admiration and criticism. Detractors argue that Musk's timelines and promises can be overly optimistic, sometimes leading to missed deadlines and investor skepticism. However, his track record of turning ambitious visions into reality cannot be overlooked.

Elon Musk's influence extends beyond his companies and technological achievements. He is known for his charismatic and sometimes controversial public persona. His active presence on social media, particularly Twitter, has made him a prominent figure in popular culture. Musk's tweets can move markets, influence public opinion, and generate significant media attention. This direct communication style has allowed him to build a strong personal brand and engage with a wide audience, although it has also led to legal challenges and scrutiny from regulatory bodies.

Musk's leadership style is often described as intense and demanding. He sets high expectations for himself and his teams, fostering a culture of innovation and excellence. His hands-on approach and willingness to delve into technical details have earned him respect from engineers and scientists, who appreciate his deep understanding of complex subjects. Musk's ability to inspire and motivate his employees has been a key factor in the success of his ventures, creating an environment where groundbreaking ideas can flourish.

Despite his many accomplishments, Musk has faced numerous challenges and setbacks throughout his career. The early days of SpaceX were fraught with financial difficulties, and Tesla came close to bankruptcy several times. Musk has openly discussed the personal toll these struggles have taken on him, including moments of extreme stress and doubt. Nevertheless, his resilience and determination have enabled him to navigate these obstacles and emerge stronger.

Musk's impact on the world extends to his philanthropic efforts. He has pledged to donate the majority of his wealth to address global challenges through the Musk Foundation, which focuses on renewable energy, space exploration, pediatric research, and science education. His contributions to science and technology are not just limited to his business ventures but also include efforts to inspire the next generation of innovators.

Chapter 24: Stephen Hawking

Stephen Hawking, one of the most brilliant theoretical physicists of our time, was born on January 8, 1942, in Oxford, England. His contributions to cosmology, general relativity, and quantum gravity, especially in the context of black holes, have profoundly influenced our understanding of the universe. Despite facing a debilitating neurodegenerative disease, Hawking's work has left an indelible mark on science and popular culture.

Hawking's early life was marked by academic curiosity and intellectual rigor. He was born into a family that placed a high value on education, with his father, Frank, being a medical researcher and his mother, Isobel, a political activist. This environment nurtured Hawking's love for learning from a young age. He attended St Albans School in Hertfordshire, where his natural aptitude for mathematics and physics became evident. However, it was during his time at University College, Oxford, where he studied physics, that Hawking's potential truly began to shine. Despite finding the coursework easy and sometimes lacking motivation, he graduated with a first-class honors degree.

In 1962, Hawking began his graduate studies at Trinity Hall, Cambridge, where he was supervised by the eminent cosmologist Dennis Sciama. It was during this period that he was diagnosed with amyotrophic lateral sclerosis (ALS), also known as Lou Gehrig's disease, at the age of 21. This diagnosis was devastating, with doctors initially giving him a prognosis of just a few years to live. Despite the physical decline that followed, Hawking's mind remained sharp and undeterred. He immersed himself in his research, determined to make significant contributions to science despite his illness.

Hawking's early work focused on singularities in the context of general relativity. Alongside Roger Penrose, he demonstrated that singularities—points where gravitational forces cause matter to have infinite density and zero volume—were not just theoretical curiosities but could arise in the real universe. This groundbreaking work provided key insights into the nature of black holes and the origins of the universe, suggesting that the universe might have begun as a singularity in the Big Bang.

One of Hawking's most significant contributions to theoretical physics was his discovery that black holes emit radiation, now known as Hawking radiation. This was a revolutionary idea because it implied that black holes, which were previously thought to be completely black and from which nothing could escape, could lose mass and energy over time. This radiation arises from quantum effects near the event horizon, the boundary beyond which nothing can return. Hawking's work on black hole thermodynamics bridged the gap between general relativity and quantum mechanics, two of the most fundamental yet seemingly incompatible theories in physics.

Hawking's theoretical innovations did not stop there. He also proposed the "no boundary" condition with James Hartle, suggesting that the universe has no boundaries in imaginary time. This idea implies that the universe is finite but unbounded, akin to the surface of a sphere. It provided a new framework for understanding the initial conditions of the universe and the nature of time itself. His work has stimulated ongoing research in cosmology and theoretical physics, challenging and refining our understanding of the cosmos.

Despite his physical limitations, Hawking became an influential public figure, known for his wit, sense of humor, and ability to communicate complex scientific ideas to a broad audience. His 1988 book, "A Brief History of Time," became an international bestseller, making intricate concepts like the Big Bang, black holes, and quantum mechanics accessible to non-specialists. The book's success brought him widespread fame and established him as a prominent voice in the public understanding of science.

Hawking's life story, characterized by his battle with ALS and his extraordinary intellectual achievements, has inspired millions. His resilience in the face of adversity, combined with his groundbreaking scientific contributions, has made him a symbol of the human spirit's capacity to overcome challenges. His work has been recognized with numerous awards and honors, including the prestigious Lucasian Professorship of Mathematics at Cambridge, a position once held by Isaac Newton.

In addition to his scientific pursuits, Hawking engaged in various public and political issues. He was an advocate for the rights of people with disabilities, often highlighting the need for better accessibility and support. He also expressed concerns about the future of humanity, particularly the risks posed by artificial intelligence and climate change. Hawking's insights and warnings about these global challenges have spurred important discussions about the ethical implications of technological advancements and the need for sustainable practices.

Hawking's influence extended into popular culture as well. He made guest appearances on television shows like "The Simpsons" and "Star Trek: The Next Generation," where he portrayed himself, further cementing his status as a cultural icon. His distinctive computerized voice, produced by a speech-generating device, became instantly recognizable and added to his unique persona. Hawking's life and work have been the subject of numerous documentaries and films, most notably the biographical drama "The Theory of Everything," which depicted his early life, academic career, and relationship with his first wife, Jane Wilde.

Throughout his career, Hawking collaborated with many leading scientists, contributing to a vast body of work that continues to influence contemporary physics. He mentored numerous students, many of whom have gone on to make significant contributions to the field. His legacy is not only reflected in his scientific papers and theories but also in the ongoing research inspired by his ideas.

Hawking's later years were marked by continued exploration of fundamental questions about the universe. He remained active in his research and public engagements until his death on March 14, 2018, a date that poignantly coincides with Pi Day and the anniversary of Albert Einstein's birth. His passing was mourned by the global scientific community and beyond, as people from all walks of life reflected on the profound impact of his work and his extraordinary life story.

Stephen Hawking's legacy is multifaceted. He expanded our understanding of black holes, cosmology, and the nature of the universe, bridging gaps between disparate fields of physics. His ability to overcome severe physical challenges while making groundbreaking scientific contributions serves as an inspiration to scientists and non-scientists alike. His work continues to influence current research and will likely do so for generations to come. As we continue to explore the mysteries of the universe, Hawking's theories and insights will remain a guiding light, reminding us of the power of human curiosity and the endless possibilities of scientific inquiry.

Chapter 25: Richard Feynman

Richard Feynman was an extraordinary physicist whose contributions to quantum mechanics, quantum electrodynamics, and the philosophy of science have left an indelible mark on the scientific community and beyond. Born on May 11, 1918, in Queens, New York, Feynman displayed an early fascination with science and an insatiable curiosity that would shape his illustrious career. His father's encouragement to ask questions and explore the natural world laid the foundation for Feynman's unconventional approach to learning and problem-solving.

Feynman's academic journey began at the Massachusetts Institute of Technology (MIT), where he pursued a degree in physics. His time at MIT was marked by intense intellectual activity and a penchant for practical jokes, showcasing his playful yet serious engagement with the world around him. After graduating from MIT, Feynman continued his studies at Princeton University, where he completed his Ph.D. under the guidance of John Wheeler. His doctoral thesis on the principle of least action in quantum mechanics set the stage for his future groundbreaking work.

During World War II, Feynman was recruited to work on the Manhattan Project at Los Alamos National Laboratory, where he played a crucial role in the development of the atomic bomb. Although he later expressed ambivalence about the use of nuclear weapons, his work at Los Alamos was characterized by innovative problem-solving and leadership. Feynman's contributions to the project, including his development of efficient methods for calculating neutron diffusion, demonstrated his ability to apply theoretical knowledge to practical challenges.

After the war, Feynman's academic career flourished. He accepted a position at Cornell University, where his teaching and research gained widespread recognition. It was during this period that he developed his path-breaking work on quantum electrodynamics (QED), which describes how light and matter interact. Feynman's development of Feynman diagrams, a graphical representation of particle interactions, revolutionized the way physicists conceptualize and calculate quantum phenomena. These diagrams simplified complex equations and provided a visual tool that has become fundamental in the field of particle physics.

Feynman's work on QED earned him the Nobel Prize in Physics in 1965, which he shared with Julian Schwinger and Sin-Itiro Tomonaga. Their collective contributions resolved inconsistencies between quantum mechanics and special relativity, providing a more complete understanding of electromagnetic interactions. Feynman's approach to QED was characterized by its intuitive and accessible nature, which contrasted with the more formal methods of his contemporaries. His ability to communicate complex ideas in a simple and engaging manner became one of his defining traits.

In 1950, Feynman moved to the California Institute of Technology (Caltech), where he continued to make significant contributions to theoretical physics. His work on the theory of superfluidity in liquid helium and his development of the parton model, which describes the behavior of quarks inside protons and neutrons, further expanded his influence in the field. Feynman's innovative ideas and methodologies often challenged conventional thinking, pushing the boundaries of scientific understanding.

Beyond his technical contributions, Feynman was renowned for his charisma and ability to inspire students and colleagues. His lectures, characterized by their clarity, humor, and passion, left a lasting impact on those who attended. The publication of "The Feynman Lectures on Physics," a comprehensive introductory physics textbook based on his lectures at Caltech, has educated generations of physicists and remains a seminal work in the field. These lectures showcased his unique teaching style, which emphasized conceptual understanding and intuitive problem-solving.

Feynman's curiosity extended beyond the confines of physics. He had a wide range of interests, including art, music, and biology. He taught himself to play the bongo drums, and his performances became a beloved aspect of his public persona. Feynman also pursued artistic endeavors, creating detailed sketches and paintings. His interdisciplinary approach to life and science exemplified his belief in the interconnectedness of knowledge and the importance of creativity in all endeavors.

One of the most famous episodes in Feynman's life was his involvement in the investigation of the Space Shuttle Challenger disaster in 1986. Appointed to the Rogers Commission, Feynman applied his rigorous scientific approach to uncover the cause of the accident. His demonstration of the O-ring's vulnerability to low temperatures, using a simple glass of ice water during a televised hearing, highlighted the importance of clear, empirical evidence in scientific inquiry. This investigation not only revealed critical flaws in NASA's safety protocols but also underscored Feynman's commitment to integrity and truth in science.

Feynman's writings and autobiographical works, including "Surely You're Joking, Mr. Feynman!" and "What Do You Care What Other People Think?", provide insights into his personality, philosophy, and approach to life. These books, filled with anecdotes and reflections, reveal his relentless curiosity, skepticism of authority, and love of adventure. Feynman's ability to convey profound scientific insights through storytelling made his works accessible to a broad audience and cemented his status as a beloved figure in both the scientific community and popular culture.

Throughout his career, Feynman received numerous accolades and honors, including the Albert Einstein Award and the National Medal of Science. Despite his many achievements, he remained humble and approachable, often downplaying his contributions and emphasizing the collective nature of scientific progress. His interactions with students and colleagues were characterized by a spirit of collaboration and mutual respect, fostering an environment of open inquiry and intellectual exploration.

Feynman's legacy extends far beyond his scientific contributions. He championed the importance of scientific literacy and education, advocating for a society that values critical thinking and empirical evidence. His passion for teaching and his ability to inspire curiosity in others have left an enduring impact on the field of education. Feynman's influence can be seen in the countless scientists he mentored and inspired, many of whom have made significant contributions to their respective fields.

Richard Feynman's life and work exemplify the essence of scientific exploration and the pursuit of knowledge. His contributions to quantum mechanics, quantum electrodynamics, and particle physics have fundamentally shaped our understanding of the universe. His ability to communicate complex ideas with clarity and enthusiasm has inspired generations of scientists and non-scientists alike. Feynman's legacy is a testament to the power of curiosity, creativity, and critical thinking in advancing human understanding.

Chapter 26: JK Rowling

J.K. Rowling, born Joanne Rowling on July 31, 1965, in Yate, Gloucestershire, England, is a British author best known for creating the globally renowned Harry Potter series. Her journey from a struggling single mother to one of the world's most successful and influential writers is a remarkable tale of resilience, creativity, and the transformative power of literature. Rowling's life story, her literary achievements, and her impact on popular culture and philanthropy are nothing short of extraordinary.

Rowling's early life was marked by a deep love for storytelling and a vivid imagination. She grew up in a modest household with her parents, Peter and Anne Rowling, and her younger sister, Dianne. From a young age, Rowling showed a keen interest in writing and often created fantastical stories to entertain herself and her family. Her passion for books was nurtured by her mother, who would read to her daughters and encourage their creative pursuits.

Rowling's academic journey took her to the University of Exeter, where she studied French and the Classics. Her time at university was formative, exposing her to a broad range of literature and honing her language skills. After graduating, Rowling moved to London, where she worked in various jobs, including a stint as a researcher and bilingual secretary for Amnesty International. These experiences provided her with a broader perspective on human rights and social issues, themes that would later be reflected in her writing.

The genesis of the Harry Potter series is the stuff of literary legend. In 1990, while on a delayed train journey from Manchester to London, the idea for Harry Potter, a young wizard attending a magical school, came to Rowling fully formed. She envisioned a world rich with magic, intrigue, and adventure, centering on a boy who discovers his true identity and destiny. The next few years were challenging for Rowling, as she faced personal hardships, including the death of her mother, a failed marriage, and the responsibilities of raising her daughter, Jessica, as a single mother.

Despite these challenges, Rowling's determination to bring her story to life never wavered. She began writing the first Harry Potter book, often working in cafes while her daughter slept beside her. Her perseverance paid off in 1997 when Bloomsbury, a relatively small publishing house, agreed to publish "Harry Potter and the Philosopher's Stone" (released as "Harry Potter and the Sorcerer's Stone" in the United States). The book was an instant success, captivating readers with its imaginative world, compelling characters, and themes of friendship, bravery, and the battle between good and evil.

The success of the first book paved the way for six sequels, creating a seven-part series that would become a global phenomenon. The Harry Potter books have been translated into over 80 languages, sold more than 500 million copies worldwide, and adapted into a blockbuster film series. Rowling's intricate plotting, richly developed characters, and the depth of the magical universe she created have earned her critical acclaim and a dedicated fan base.

One of the defining features of Rowling's writing is her ability to blend fantasy with real-world issues. The Harry Potter series addresses themes such as prejudice, corruption, the abuse of power, and the importance of choice and personal integrity. These themes resonate with readers of all ages, making the books not only entertaining but also thought-provoking. Characters like Harry Potter, Hermione Granger, and Ron Weasley have become cultural icons, embodying values of courage, loyalty, and perseverance.

Rowling's impact extends beyond the literary world. The success of the Harry Potter series has had a significant influence on popular culture, inspiring a wide range of merchandise, theme parks, and fan communities. The Wizarding World of Harry Potter attractions at Universal Studios theme parks have brought Rowling's magical universe to life, allowing fans to immerse themselves in the world she created. Additionally, the series has inspired a new generation of readers, contributing to a resurgence of interest in children's literature and fantasy fiction.

In addition to the main Harry Potter series, Rowling has expanded the Wizarding World with spin-off works and related projects. "Fantastic Beasts and Where to Find Them," originally a fictional textbook within the Harry Potter universe, was developed into a film series exploring the adventures of Newt Scamander, a magizoologist in the early 20th century. This expansion of the Harry Potter universe has allowed Rowling to explore new stories and characters while maintaining the magic and charm that captivated readers in the original series.

Rowling's success has also enabled her to engage in significant philanthropic efforts. She established the Volant Charitable Trust, which supports a wide range of causes, including research into multiple sclerosis (a disease that affected her mother), anti-poverty initiatives, and children's welfare. Rowling is also a co-founder of Lumos, a nonprofit organization dedicated to ending the institutionalization of children worldwide and promoting community-based care. Her charitable work reflects her commitment to social justice and her desire to use her success to make a positive impact on the world.

Despite her achievements, Rowling has faced criticism and controversy, particularly related to her comments on social media and her views on gender identity and transgender issues. These controversies have sparked intense debate and backlash, highlighting the complexities and challenges of navigating public life as a prominent figure. Rowling's responses to criticism have varied, with some defending her right to express her views and others calling for greater sensitivity and understanding of the impact of her words.

In addition to her work in the Wizarding World, Rowling has ventured into writing for adults under the pseudonym Robert

Galbraith. The Cormoran Strike series, a set of crime fiction novels, follows the investigations of private detective Cormoran Strike and his partner, Robin Ellacott. These books have been well-received, showcasing Rowling's versatility as a writer and her ability to craft compelling narratives across different genres.

Rowling's personal life has also evolved over the years. She married Neil Murray, a doctor, in 2001, and the couple has two children together, David and Mackenzie. Balancing her family life with her writing and philanthropic activities, Rowling has continued to be a prominent figure in both the literary world and public discourse.

Rowling's journey from a struggling writer to a global literary icon is a testament to the power of perseverance, imagination, and the transformative impact of storytelling. Her creation of the Harry Potter series has left an indelible mark on literature and popular culture, inspiring millions of readers around the world. Through her writing, philanthropy, and public engagement, Rowling has demonstrated the ability to influence and inspire across multiple spheres.

Chapter 27: George Lucas

George Lucas, born on May 14, 1944, in Modesto, California, is a filmmaker, screenwriter, producer, and entrepreneur whose contributions to cinema and popular culture have been profound and far-reaching. As the creator of the "Star Wars" and "Indiana Jones" franchises, Lucas has left an indelible mark on the film industry, pushing the boundaries of technology, storytelling, and merchandising. His visionary approach to filmmaking has influenced generations of filmmakers and transformed the landscape of modern cinema.

Lucas's early life in Modesto was marked by a love of cars and racing, a passion that would later influence his work. He initially aspired to be a race car driver but changed his career path after a near-fatal car accident. During his recovery, Lucas developed an interest in photography and filmmaking. He attended Modesto Junior College, where he studied anthropology, sociology, and literature, and became increasingly involved in film and photography.

In 1966, Lucas transferred to the University of Southern California's School of Cinematic Arts, one of the most prestigious film schools in the United States. There, he honed his skills in filmmaking and developed a distinctive visual style. His student films, including the award-winning "Electronic Labyrinth: THX 1138 4EB," showcased his talent for innovative storytelling and visual effects. This early work laid the groundwork for his future successes and established him as a promising young filmmaker.

Lucas's first feature film, "THX 1138," was released in 1971. Adapted from his student film, it is a dystopian science fiction story that explores themes of individuality and control in a futuristic society. Though not a commercial success at the time, "THX 1138" demonstrated Lucas's ambition and willingness to take creative risks.

The film's distinctive visual style and use of special effects foreshadowed the groundbreaking work that would define his career.

Lucas's breakthrough came with the release of "American Graffiti" in 1973. The film, set in the early 1960s, is a nostalgic look at teenage life and car culture in a small American town. "American Graffiti" was a critical and commercial success, earning five Academy Award nominations, including Best Picture and Best Director. The film's success provided Lucas with the financial and creative freedom to pursue his next project, a space opera inspired by the serials and adventure films of his youth.

The development of "Star Wars" was a monumental undertaking that would change the course of film history. Lucas began writing the screenplay in the early 1970s, drawing inspiration from a wide range of sources, including mythology, classical literature, and the work of Joseph Campbell, whose concept of the "monomyth" or "hero's journey" became a central framework for the story. The original "Star Wars" trilogy, later known as "Star Wars: Episode IV – A New Hope," was released in 1977.

"Star Wars" was a revolutionary film that redefined the science fiction genre and set new standards for special effects, sound design, and production values. The film's groundbreaking use of visual effects, created by Lucas's company Industrial Light & Magic (ILM), set a new benchmark for the industry. ILM pioneered techniques such as computer-generated imagery (CGI) and motion control photography, which became staples of modern filmmaking. The success of "Star Wars" spawned two sequels, "The Empire Strikes Back" (1980) and "Return of the Jedi" (1983), both of which were critical and commercial successes.

Lucas's creation of the "Star Wars" universe extended beyond the films themselves. He recognized the potential for a vast transmedia narrative that included books, comics, video games, and television series. This approach not only expanded the story but also established a model for franchise development that has been emulated by numerous other properties. The "Star Wars" franchise became a cultural phenomenon, with an enduring fan base and a pervasive influence on popular culture.

In addition to the "Star Wars" saga, Lucas created another iconic film series with the "Indiana Jones" franchise. Collaborating with director Steven Spielberg, Lucas co-wrote and produced "Raiders of the Lost Ark" (1981), which introduced audiences to the adventurous archaeologist Indiana Jones, played by Harrison Ford. The film was a critical and commercial success, leading to three sequels: "Indiana Jones and the Temple of Doom" (1984), "Indiana Jones and the Last Crusade" (1989), and "Indiana Jones and the Kingdom of the Crystal Skull" (2008). The series combined thrilling action, humor, and historical fantasy, further cementing Lucas's reputation as a master storyteller.

Lucas's impact on the film industry extends beyond his work as a filmmaker. He is a pioneering entrepreneur who has revolutionized film technology and production processes. In 1975, he founded Industrial Light & Magic (ILM) to create the special effects for "Star Wars." ILM became the leading visual effects company in the world, contributing to numerous blockbuster films and advancing the art and science of visual effects. Lucas also founded Skywalker Sound, a state-of-the-art sound design and post-production facility, and Lucasfilm, which became one of the most successful independent production companies in the industry.

In 1983, Lucas founded the animation studio Lucasfilm Animation and later launched the successful "Star Wars: The Clone Wars" television series. His vision for creating high-quality animation and pushing the boundaries of storytelling in the medium further demonstrated his commitment to innovation. Lucas's work in animation paved the way for advancements in CGI and digital filmmaking, influencing the development of animated films and television series across the industry.

Lucas's contributions to film technology and innovation were recognized with numerous awards and honors. He received the Irving G. Thalberg Memorial Award from the Academy of Motion Picture Arts and Sciences in 1991, the American Film Institute's Lifetime Achievement Award in 2005, and the National Medal of Arts in 2013. These accolades reflect his enduring influence on the film industry and his role as a visionary leader in the field.

In 2012, Lucas made a significant decision to sell Lucasfilm to The Walt Disney Company for over $4 billion. This move ensured the continuation and expansion of the "Star Wars" franchise, with Disney producing new films, television series, and other media. The sale also allowed Lucas to focus on his philanthropic efforts and personal projects. He established the George Lucas Educational Foundation, which supports innovative educational initiatives and promotes the use of technology in education. Through his foundation and other charitable endeavors, Lucas has contributed to improving education and fostering creativity and critical thinking among students.

Lucas's philanthropic efforts extend to the arts, health, and social justice. He and his wife, Mellody Hobson, have made substantial donations to various causes, including a $10 million endowment to the University of Southern California's School of Cinematic Arts and a $25 million donation to the Chicago-based non-profit organization After School Matters. Their commitment to giving back reflects Lucas's belief in the power of education and the importance of providing opportunities for future generations.

Lucas's influence on the film industry and popular culture is immeasurable. His pioneering work in special effects, sound design, and digital filmmaking has set new standards and inspired countless filmmakers. The "Star Wars" and "Indiana Jones" franchises have become cultural touchstones, beloved by audiences worldwide and continuing to captivate new generations of fans. Lucas's commitment to innovation, storytelling, and philanthropy has left a lasting legacy that extends far beyond his cinematic achievements.

Chapter 28: Steven Spielberg

Steven Spielberg, born on December 18, 1946, in Cincinnati, Ohio, is one of the most influential and successful filmmakers in the history of cinema. His career spans over five decades, during which he has directed, produced, and written some of the most iconic films of all time. Spielberg's work has not only defined genres but also pushed the boundaries of filmmaking technology, storytelling, and cultural impact. His extraordinary vision, creativity, and dedication to his craft have earned him a place among the greatest directors in the annals of film history.

Spielberg's early life was marked by a profound love for movies and storytelling. Raised in a Jewish family, he faced antisemitism and moved frequently due to his father's job as an electrical engineer. These experiences of alienation and displacement often influenced the themes of his films, particularly the sense of wonder, belonging, and the importance of family. Spielberg's fascination with cinema began at a young age, and he started making short films with his father's 8mm camera. His early experiments in filmmaking included stop-motion animation and rudimentary special effects, showcasing his burgeoning talent and passion for visual storytelling.

Spielberg's formal education in filmmaking began at California State University, Long Beach, where he majored in film production. However, it was his internship at Universal Studios that proved to be a turning point in his career. He caught the attention of studio executives with his short film "Amblin'" (1968), a 26-minute film that won several awards and led to a contract with Universal. Spielberg became the youngest director ever to be signed to a long-term deal with a major Hollywood studio.

Spielberg's early work in television included directing episodes of popular shows such as "Columbo" and "Marcus Welby, M.D." His big break came with the made-for-TV movie "Duel" (1971), a tense thriller about a man being chased by a mysterious truck on a deserted highway. The film's success showcased Spielberg's ability to create suspense and garnered critical acclaim, paving the way for his transition to feature films.

Spielberg's first theatrical release was "The Sugarland Express" (1974), a crime drama based on a true story. Despite its modest success, it was his next film, "Jaws" (1975), that catapulted him to international fame. "Jaws," a thriller about a great white shark terrorizing a small New England beach town, became a massive box office hit and is credited with creating the summer blockbuster phenomenon. The film's innovative use of suspense, special effects, and John Williams' iconic score made it a landmark in cinema history.

Following the success of "Jaws," Spielberg directed "Close Encounters of the Third Kind" (1977), a science fiction film about humans making contact with extraterrestrial life. The film was another critical and commercial success, further establishing Spielberg's reputation as a master storyteller with a unique ability to blend spectacle with emotional depth. His portrayal of awe and wonder in "Close Encounters" resonated with audiences and highlighted his distinctive approach to filmmaking.

Spielberg's next major project was "Raiders of the Lost Ark" (1981), the first film in the Indiana Jones series, which he co-created with George Lucas. Starring Harrison Ford as the adventurous archaeologist Indiana Jones, the film combined action, humor, and romance in a thrilling homage to the serials of the 1930s and 1940s. "Raiders of the Lost Ark" was a critical and commercial triumph, leading to three sequels: "Indiana Jones and the Temple of Doom" (1984), "Indiana Jones and the Last Crusade" (1989), and "Indiana Jones and the Kingdom of the Crystal Skull" (2008). The series cemented Spielberg's status as a premier director of blockbuster entertainment.

In 1982, Spielberg directed "E.T. the Extra-Terrestrial," a heartfelt story about a young boy who befriends an alien stranded on Earth. The film was a cultural phenomenon, becoming the highest-grossing film of all time until it was surpassed by "Jurassic Park" (1993), another Spielberg-directed film. "E.T." was praised for its emotional resonance, innovative special effects, and the compelling performance of its young cast. It remains one of Spielberg's most beloved films, embodying his recurring themes of childhood wonder and the power of friendship.

Spielberg's versatility as a filmmaker is evident in his diverse body of work. In addition to his success with science fiction and adventure films, he has tackled historical dramas, war films, and biographical works with equal skill. "The Color Purple" (1985), based on Alice Walker's Pulitzer Prize-winning novel, marked Spielberg's first foray into serious drama. The film, which deals with themes of racism, sexism, and redemption, received critical acclaim and numerous Academy Award nominations, showcasing Spielberg's ability to handle complex and sensitive subjects.

Spielberg continued to explore historical themes with "Empire of the Sun" (1987), based on J.G. Ballard's semi-autobiographical novel about a young boy's experiences during World War II in Japanese-occupied China. The film, though not as commercially successful as some of his previous works, was praised for its epic scope, visual splendor, and the performance of its young star, Christian Bale. Spielberg's commitment to authenticity and emotional truth in historical narratives became a hallmark of his later work.

In 1993, Spielberg achieved a remarkable feat by releasing two of his most acclaimed films in the same year: "Jurassic Park" and "Schindler's List." "Jurassic Park," based on Michael Crichton's novel, revolutionized the use of computer-generated imagery (CGI) and animatronics to bring dinosaurs to life on the big screen. The film's groundbreaking visual effects, thrilling action sequences, and engaging story made it a box office sensation and a pivotal moment in the history of visual effects.

"Schindler's List," on the other hand, was a stark and harrowing portrayal of the Holocaust, based on the true story of Oskar Schindler, a German businessman who saved over a thousand Jews from extermination. Filmed in black and white, the movie was a deeply personal project for Spielberg, who is Jewish and had family members affected by the Holocaust. "Schindler's List" received widespread critical acclaim and won seven Academy Awards, including Best Picture and Best Director. The film's impact on audiences and its role in Holocaust education and remembrance are testaments to Spielberg's commitment to telling powerful, socially relevant stories.

Following the success of "Schindler's List," Spielberg established the USC Shoah Foundation, an organization dedicated to recording and preserving testimonies of Holocaust survivors and other genocide witnesses. The foundation's work in education and awareness has had a significant global impact, reflecting Spielberg's dedication to using his influence for social good.

Spielberg continued to explore diverse genres and themes throughout the 1990s and 2000s. "Amistad" (1997) depicted the true story of a mutiny on a slave ship and the subsequent legal battle, highlighting issues of justice and human rights. "Saving Private Ryan" (1998), a visceral and realistic portrayal of the D-Day invasion during World War II, was praised for its groundbreaking battle scenes and emotional depth. The film won several Academy Awards, including Best Director for Spielberg, and is considered one of the greatest war films ever made.

In the 2000s, Spielberg ventured into science fiction again with "A.I. Artificial Intelligence" (2001) and "Minority Report" (2002), both of which explored futuristic themes and ethical dilemmas. "A.I.," based on a project initiated by Stanley Kubrick, delved into the relationship between humans and artificial beings, while "Minority

Report," based on a Philip K. Dick story, examined issues of free will and pre-crime technology. These films demonstrated Spielberg's continued interest in speculative fiction and his ability to tackle complex philosophical questions.

Spielberg also revisited historical drama with "Munich" (2005), which depicted the aftermath of the 1972 Munich Olympics massacre and the Israeli government's response. The film was both critically acclaimed and controversial, praised for its balanced portrayal of a sensitive subject and its exploration of the moral ambiguities of vengeance and justice.

In 2012, Spielberg directed "Lincoln," a biographical drama about President Abraham Lincoln's efforts to pass the Thirteenth Amendment and end slavery in the United States. The film, anchored by Daniel Day-Lewis's Oscar-winning performance, was a critical and commercial success, earning numerous awards and accolades. "Lincoln" showcased Spielberg's skill in historical storytelling and his ability to bring nuanced, character-driven narratives to the screen.

Spielberg's influence extends beyond his work as a director. He co-founded Amblin Entertainment, a production company that has produced numerous successful films and television series, including "Back to the Future" (1985), "The Goonies" (1985), "Who Framed Roger Rabbit" (1988), and "Jurassic Park." In 1994, Spielberg co-founded DreamWorks SKG with Jeffrey Katzenberg and David Geffen, aiming to create a filmmaker-friendly studio. DreamWorks produced a wide range of critically acclaimed and commercially successful films, further cementing Spielberg's status as a powerful force in Hollywood.

Spielberg's contributions to the film industry have been recognized with numerous awards and honors. He has received multiple Academy Awards, Golden Globes, and BAFTA Awards, as well as the AFI Life Achievement Award, the Kennedy Center Honors, and the Presidential Medal of Freedom. These accolades reflect his unparalleled impact on cinema and his enduring legacy as one of the greatest filmmakers of all time.

In addition to his filmmaking achievements, Spielberg has been a prominent advocate for film preservation and education. He has supported initiatives to restore and preserve classic films, ensuring that future generations can experience the rich history of cinema. Spielberg's dedication to nurturing young talent and fostering a love of filmmaking is evident in his involvement with film schools and mentorship programs.

Spielberg's personal life has also been marked by a commitment to family and philanthropy. He has been married to actress Kate Capshaw since 1991, and the couple has seven children. Together, they have supported numerous charitable causes, including education, healthcare, and the arts. Spielberg's philanthropic efforts reflect his belief in giving back to the community and using his influence to make a positive impact on the world.

Chapter 29: Stanley Kubrick

Stanley Kubrick, born on July 26, 1928, in the Bronx, New York City, was a filmmaker, screenwriter, and producer renowned for his meticulous craftsmanship, intellectual depth, and ability to span various genres. Throughout his career, Kubrick created some of the most influential and critically acclaimed films in the history of cinema, establishing himself as a visionary auteur whose works continue to inspire and challenge audiences and filmmakers alike.

Kubrick's interest in the arts began at an early age. His father, Jacques Kubrick, a doctor, encouraged his intellectual pursuits and gave him a camera when he was twelve years old. Kubrick quickly developed a passion for photography, spending hours taking pictures around New York City. By the time he was seventeen, he was working as a staff photographer for Look magazine, where he honed his skills in composition, lighting, and storytelling through images. This early experience with photography profoundly influenced his visual style as a filmmaker.

Kubrick's transition to filmmaking started with short documentaries. His first, "Day of the Fight" (1951), was a short film about middleweight boxer Walter Cartier, which showcased Kubrick's ability to create tension and drama within a documentary format. Encouraged by its success, he made two more short documentaries, "Flying Padre" (1951) and "The Seafarers" (1953), before deciding to venture into feature films.

Kubrick's first feature film, "Fear and Desire" (1953), was an independently financed project that explored the psychological effects of war. Although it was not a commercial success, it demonstrated Kubrick's potential and determination as a filmmaker. His next film, "Killer's Kiss" (1955), was a noir thriller that further showcased his talent for creating atmospheric tension and complex characters. Despite its modest budget and limited release, "Killer's Kiss" caught the attention of producers and critics, leading to more opportunities in Hollywood.

Kubrick's breakthrough came with "The Killing" (1956), a heist film that displayed his mastery of narrative structure and visual storytelling. The film, produced by James B. Harris, was praised for its innovative use of non-linear narrative and intricate plot, drawing comparisons to the works of Alfred Hitchcock and John Huston. "The Killing" established Kubrick as a rising star in the industry and led to his collaboration with Harris on several subsequent projects.

In 1957, Kubrick directed "Paths of Glory," a World War I drama based on Humphrey Cobb's novel. Starring Kirk Douglas, the film depicted the moral and ethical dilemmas faced by soldiers and officers in the French army. "Paths of Glory" was a critical success, praised for its powerful performances, stark cinematography, and anti-war message. It remains one of the most compelling war films ever made, reflecting Kubrick's ability to blend powerful storytelling with profound philosophical questions.

Kubrick's next major project was "Spartacus" (1960), a historical epic about the slave revolt led by the titular character. The film, produced by and starring Kirk Douglas, was a massive production that faced numerous challenges, including creative differences between Douglas and the original director, Anthony Mann. Kubrick was brought in to replace Mann and bring the film to completion. Despite the production difficulties, "Spartacus" was a commercial and critical success, winning four Academy Awards and solidifying Kubrick's reputation as a director capable of handling large-scale projects.

However, Kubrick's experience on "Spartacus" also reinforced his desire for creative control over his films. Frustrated by the limitations imposed by studio systems, he moved to England, where he would spend the rest of his career working independently. This move allowed him to maintain full artistic control over his projects, resulting in some of the most innovative and influential films in cinema history.

Kubrick's first film after relocating to England was "Lolita" (1962), an adaptation of Vladimir Nabokov's controversial novel about a middle-aged man's obsession with a teenage girl. The film faced significant challenges due to its provocative subject matter and the strict censorship laws of the time. Despite these obstacles, Kubrick crafted a film that balanced dark humor with unsettling drama, earning critical acclaim and further establishing his reputation as a daring and innovative filmmaker.

Following "Lolita," Kubrick embarked on one of his most ambitious projects, "Dr. Strangelove or: How I Learned to Stop Worrying and Love the Bomb" (1964). This satirical black comedy about nuclear war and Cold War politics showcased Kubrick's ability to blend humor with biting social commentary. The film, starring Peter Sellers in multiple roles, was a critical and commercial success, praised for its sharp wit, innovative visual style, and bold narrative. "Dr. Strangelove" remains one of Kubrick's most enduring and influential works, reflecting his unique ability to tackle serious themes with dark humor and intellectual rigor.

Kubrick's next film, "2001: A Space Odyssey" (1968), is widely regarded as one of the greatest and most influential films ever made. Based on a short story by Arthur C. Clarke, who co-wrote the screenplay with Kubrick, the film explores themes of human evolution, artificial intelligence, and the mysteries of space. "2001: A Space Odyssey" was groundbreaking in its use of special effects, innovative visual techniques, and the integration of classical music into its soundtrack. The film's enigmatic narrative and philosophical depth challenged audiences and critics, earning a place as a seminal work in the science fiction genre and a testament to Kubrick's visionary approach to filmmaking.

Following the success of "2001," Kubrick continued to explore diverse genres and complex themes. "A Clockwork Orange" (1971), based on Anthony Burgess's novel, delved into the nature of violence, free will, and societal control. The film's depiction of ultraviolence and its stylized, dystopian world sparked controversy and debate, leading to censorship and bans in several countries. Despite the controversy, "A Clockwork Orange" was critically acclaimed and has since become a cult classic, recognized for its provocative themes, innovative visual style, and compelling performances.

In 1975, Kubrick directed "Barry Lyndon," a period drama based on William Makepeace Thackeray's novel. The film, set in the 18th century, follows the rise and fall of an Irish adventurer. "Barry Lyndon" was notable for its meticulous attention to historical detail, including the use of natural lighting and candlelight to achieve a painterly visual style. Although it was not a commercial success at the time, "Barry Lyndon" has since been reevaluated and praised for its visual beauty, narrative complexity, and Kubrick's masterful direction.

Kubrick returned to the horror genre with "The Shining" (1980), an adaptation of Stephen King's novel. The film, starring Jack Nicholson as the tormented writer Jack Torrance, is renowned for its atmospheric tension, unsettling imagery, and psychological depth. "The Shining" received mixed reviews upon its release but has since been recognized as a masterpiece of horror cinema, with its iconic scenes and haunting performances leaving a lasting impact on the genre.

In 1987, Kubrick directed "Full Metal Jacket," a war film based on Gustav Hasford's novel "The Short-Timers." The film, which depicts the brutal training of Marine recruits and the horrors of the Vietnam War, was praised for its unflinching portrayal of war and its dehumanizing effects. "Full Metal Jacket" showcased Kubrick's ability to capture the psychological and emotional complexities of his characters, as well as his skill in creating powerful and memorable cinematic images.

Kubrick's final film, "Eyes Wide Shut" (1999), was released posthumously. Based on Arthur Schnitzler's novella "Traumnovelle," the film stars Tom Cruise and Nicole Kidman as a married couple navigating themes of fidelity, desire, and psychological exploration. "Eyes Wide Shut" was notable for its dreamlike atmosphere, intricate narrative, and Kubrick's meticulous attention to detail. The film received mixed reviews but has since been appreciated for its depth, complexity, and Kubrick's signature visual style.

Throughout his career, Kubrick was known for his exacting standards and meticulous approach to filmmaking. He was involved in every aspect of his films, from scripting and cinematography to editing and production design. Kubrick's dedication to his craft often resulted in long production schedules and numerous takes to achieve the desired perfection. This level of control and attention to detail ensured that each of his films was a unique and carefully crafted work of art.

Kubrick's influence on cinema is profound and far-reaching. His innovative use of visual storytelling, groundbreaking special effects, and exploration of complex themes have inspired generations of filmmakers. Directors such as Steven Spielberg, Martin Scorsese, Christopher Nolan, and David Fincher have cited Kubrick as a significant influence on their work. His ability to seamlessly blend artistic expression with commercial appeal set a new standard for filmmakers and expanded the possibilities of what cinema could achieve.

Kubrick's films often explore themes of human nature, societal structures, and the consequences of technological advancement. His works challenge audiences to confront uncomfortable truths and question their assumptions about the world. Whether through the dystopian future of "A Clockwork Orange," the existential questions of "2001: A Space Odyssey," or the psychological horror of "The Shining," Kubrick's films provoke thought and discussion, leaving a lasting impact on viewers.

In addition to his filmmaking achievements, Kubrick's contributions to the technical aspects of cinema are significant. He pioneered new techniques in special effects, cinematography, and sound design, pushing the boundaries of what was possible in film. His collaboration with visual effects artists, composers, and other creative professionals resulted in innovative and groundbreaking work that continues to influence the industry.

Kubrick's legacy extends beyond his films. He left behind a wealth of knowledge and inspiration for future generations of filmmakers, scholars, and cinephiles. His meticulous research, attention to detail, and commitment to artistic integrity serve as a model for those who seek to create meaningful and impactful cinema. The Stanley Kubrick Archive, housed at the University of the Arts London, contains a vast collection of materials related to his life and work, providing valuable insights into his creative process and contributions to film history.

Stanley Kubrick passed away on March 7, 1999, at the age of seventy, leaving behind a body of work that continues to be studied, analyzed, and celebrated. His films remain timeless, resonating with new audiences and inspiring filmmakers around the world. Kubrick's ability to blend intellectual rigor with cinematic artistry set him apart as one of the greatest directors in the history of cinema, and his influence will be felt for generations to come.

Chapter 30: Alfred Hitchcock

Alfred Hitchcock, born on August 13, 1899, in Leytonstone, London, is often regarded as one of the most influential and iconic filmmakers in the history of cinema. Known as the "Master of Suspense," Hitchcock's prolific career spanned over six decades, during which he directed more than fifty feature films that explored themes of psychological tension, fear, and the macabre. His distinctive style, innovative techniques, and mastery of narrative form have left an indelible mark on the world of filmmaking and have cemented his legacy as a true auteur.

Hitchcock's early life and upbringing played a significant role in shaping his artistic sensibilities. He was the youngest of three children in a devoutly Catholic family, which instilled in him a sense of guilt and fear that would later permeate his work. His father, William Hitchcock, was a greengrocer, and his mother, Emma, was a homemaker. As a child, Hitchcock was often isolated and introverted, preferring to observe the world around him rather than participate actively in it. This keen sense of observation and fascination with human behavior would become a hallmark of his films.

Hitchcock's formal education began at St. Ignatius' College, a Jesuit grammar school, where he developed a love for literature and art. After completing his education, he attended the London County Council School of Engineering and Navigation, where he studied engineering and navigation. However, his passion for cinema soon led him to pursue a career in the burgeoning British film industry. In 1920, Hitchcock joined the Famous Players-Lasky studio as a title designer for silent films. His talent and creativity quickly earned him a reputation, and he soon began working as an assistant director, scriptwriter, and art director.

Hitchcock's first directorial effort came in 1925 with "The Pleasure Garden," a silent film that showcased his emerging style and narrative techniques. This was followed by "The Lodger: A Story of the London

Fog" (1927), which is often considered his first true "Hitchcockian" film. "The Lodger" introduced many of the themes and stylistic elements that would define his later work, including suspenseful storytelling, atmospheric tension, and the concept of the "wrong man" falsely accused of a crime.

The success of "The Lodger" established Hitchcock as a rising talent in the British film industry, and he continued to hone his craft with a series of films throughout the late 1920s and early 1930s. These included "Blackmail" (1929), Britain's first "talkie," and "The Man Who Knew Too Much" (1934), which marked the beginning of his collaboration with screenwriter Charles Bennett. "The Man Who Knew Too Much" was a critical and commercial success, solidifying Hitchcock's reputation as a master of suspense.

Hitchcock's growing prominence in the film industry attracted the attention of Hollywood, and in 1939, he moved to the United States under contract with producer David O. Selznick. His first American film, "Rebecca" (1940), was a gothic thriller based on Daphne du Maurier's novel. The film was a critical and commercial success, winning the Academy Award for Best Picture and earning Hitchcock his first nomination for Best Director. "Rebecca" set the stage for Hitchcock's Hollywood career and showcased his ability to blend suspense with complex character-driven narratives.

Throughout the 1940s and 1950s, Hitchcock directed a string of successful films that further established his reputation as the "Master of Suspense." These included "Suspicion" (1941), "Shadow of a Doubt" (1943), "Notorious" (1946), "Rope" (1948), "Strangers on a Train" (1951), "Dial M for Murder" (1954), "Rear Window" (1954), "To Catch a Thief" (1955), and "The Man Who Knew Too Much" (1956). Each of these films demonstrated Hitchcock's mastery of visual storytelling, innovative use of camera techniques, and ability to create tension and suspense.

One of Hitchcock's most iconic and influential films from this period is "Rear Window," which starred James Stewart and Grace Kelly. The film centers on a wheelchair-bound photographer who suspects that his neighbor has committed murder. "Rear Window" is a brilliant exploration of voyeurism, paranoia, and the nature of human observation. Hitchcock's use of a single location and point-of-view shots created a claustrophobic atmosphere that heightened the suspense and showcased his ability to manipulate audience perception.

In 1958, Hitchcock directed "Vertigo," a psychological thriller starring James Stewart and Kim Novak. "Vertigo" is often considered one of Hitchcock's masterpieces and is renowned for its complex narrative, innovative camera techniques, and exploration of themes such as obsession, identity, and deception. The film's use of color, dream sequences, and the famous "dolly zoom" shot, which creates a disorienting effect, demonstrated Hitchcock's technical prowess and artistic vision. Although "Vertigo" received mixed reviews upon its initial release, it has since been re-evaluated and is now regarded as one of the greatest films of all time.

Hitchcock's most famous and culturally significant film is undoubtedly "Psycho" (1960). Based on Robert Bloch's novel and starring Anthony Perkins, Janet Leigh, and Vera Miles, "Psycho" is a groundbreaking thriller that redefined the horror genre. The film's shocking and violent content, particularly the infamous shower scene, challenged contemporary norms and censorship standards. Hitchcock's use of innovative editing, music, and camera techniques created an atmosphere of intense suspense and terror. "Psycho" was a critical and commercial success, and its influence on the horror genre and popular culture is immeasurable.

Following "Psycho," Hitchcock continued to direct a series of successful films, including "The Birds" (1963), "Marnie" (1964), "Torn Curtain" (1966), "Topaz" (1969), "Frenzy" (1972), and "Family Plot" (1976). "The Birds," in particular, is notable for its innovative use of special effects and its exploration of primal fears and environmental themes. The film's portrayal of a small town under siege by flocks of aggressive birds created a sense of escalating terror and demonstrated Hitchcock's ability to evoke fear through seemingly ordinary elements.

Throughout his career, Hitchcock was known for his meticulous attention to detail and his innovative approach to filmmaking. He was a pioneer in the use of storyboarding, meticulously planning each shot and sequence before filming. This allowed him to maintain tight control over the visual and narrative aspects of his films. Hitchcock's use of the camera as a narrative tool, his manipulation of audience expectations, and his innovative techniques, such as the use of long takes and subjective point-of-view shots, set new standards for the art of filmmaking.

Hitchcock's films often explored themes of voyeurism, guilt, and the duality of human nature. He was fascinated by the darker aspects of the human psyche and frequently depicted characters who were caught in morally ambiguous situations. His films often featured ordinary people thrust into extraordinary circumstances, grappling with issues of identity, deception, and the consequences of their actions. Hitchcock's ability to blend psychological depth with thrilling suspense made his films both intellectually stimulating and emotionally engaging.

In addition to his technical and thematic innovations, Hitchcock was a master of audience manipulation. He understood the importance of creating suspense through careful pacing, the use of silence, and the strategic withholding of information. His famous concept of "the MacGuffin"—an object or plot device that drives the story forward but is ultimately insignificant—allowed him to focus on character development and psychological tension rather than the mechanics of the plot. This approach kept audiences on the edge of their seats and made his films compelling and unpredictable.

Hitchcock's influence extended beyond the realm of cinema. He became a cultural icon, known for his distinctive profile, witty public persona, and his appearances in brief cameos in most of his films. These cameos became a signature element of his work, adding a playful touch to his meticulously crafted narratives. Hitchcock's popularity was further cemented by his television series, "Alfred Hitchcock Presents," which aired from 1955 to 1965. The series, which featured suspenseful and often darkly humorous stories, brought Hitchcock into the homes of millions of viewers and showcased his talent for storytelling in a different medium.

Despite his immense success, Hitchcock's career was not without controversy and challenges. His demanding and exacting nature often led to tensions with actors and collaborators. He was known for his strict control over his productions and his sometimes unorthodox methods of directing, which could be both inspiring and intimidating. Some of his working relationships, particularly with actresses such as Tippi Hedren, who starred in "The Birds" and "Marnie," were marked by allegations of mistreatment and manipulation. These controversies have led to a more nuanced and critical examination of Hitchcock's legacy in recent years.

Hitchcock's contributions to cinema have been recognized with numerous awards and honors. He received the American Film Institute's Life Achievement Award in 1979 and was knighted by Queen Elizabeth II in 1980, shortly before his death. Despite being nominated five times for the Academy Award for Best Director, Hitchcock never won a competitive Oscar, a fact often cited as one of the Academy's greatest oversights. However, his influence and legacy far surpass the recognition of any single award.

Alfred Hitchcock passed away on April 29, 1980, at the age of eighty. His death marked the end of an era in filmmaking, but his work continues to inspire and influence directors, writers, and audiences around the world. Hitchcock's films remain timeless, their innovative techniques, and compelling narratives still resonating with contemporary viewers. His ability to blend artistic expression with commercial appeal set a new standard for filmmakers and expanded the possibilities of what cinema could achieve.

In the years since his death, Hitchcock's legacy has only grown stronger. Film scholars and critics continue to study and analyze his work, uncovering new layers of meaning and significance. Retrospectives, exhibitions, and restorations of his films ensure that his contributions to cinema are preserved and celebrated for future generations. Hitchcock's impact on the art of filmmaking is immeasurable, and his influence can be seen in the work of countless directors who have followed in his footsteps.

Directors such as Martin Scorsese, Steven Spielberg, Brian De Palma, and Christopher Nolan have cited Hitchcock as a major influence on their work, and his techniques and themes continue to be referenced and reinterpreted in contemporary cinema. Hitchcock's mastery of suspense, his innovative use of the camera, and his exploration of the human psyche set a benchmark for what cinema could achieve, and his legacy as the "Master of Suspense" remains unmatched.

Chapter 31: Akira Kurosawa

Akira Kurosawa, born on March 23, 1910, in Tokyo, Japan, is widely regarded as one of the greatest filmmakers in the history of cinema. His influence extends far beyond his home country, having shaped the techniques, narratives, and aesthetic sensibilities of filmmakers worldwide. Kurosawa's work spans five decades and includes a diverse range of genres, from samurai epics to contemporary dramas, each marked by his distinctive style and profound exploration of human nature.

Kurosawa was born into a samurai family, the youngest of eight children. His father, Isamu, was a former army officer and a physical education instructor, and his mother, Shima, was a housewife. Growing up, Kurosawa was exposed to both traditional Japanese culture and Western influences, thanks to his father's appreciation for Western sports and cinema. This duality would later play a significant role in shaping his cinematic vision, blending Eastern and Western storytelling techniques and aesthetics.

Kurosawa's early interest in the arts was nurtured by his older brother Heigo, who worked as a benshi, a narrator for silent films, and a theater critic. Heigo introduced Kurosawa to literature, theater, and cinema, sparking his passion for storytelling. However, Heigo's tragic suicide in 1933 deeply affected Kurosawa and influenced the themes of loss, suffering, and existential inquiry that would permeate his films.

Kurosawa began his career in the film industry in the mid-1930s, joining the Photo Chemical Laboratories, which later became Toho Studios, as an assistant director. Under the mentorship of directors such as Kajirō Yamamoto, Kurosawa honed his skills in screenwriting, editing, and directing. His directorial debut came in 1943 with "Sanshiro Sugata," a judo film that showcased his talent for dynamic action sequences and character development. Despite the wartime censorship, the film was a success and established Kurosawa as a promising new voice in Japanese cinema.

One of Kurosawa's earliest masterpieces is "Rashomon" (1950), a film that brought him international acclaim and introduced Japanese cinema to the Western world. "Rashomon" tells the story of a crime from multiple perspectives, each presenting a different version of the truth. This narrative structure, combined with Kurosawa's innovative use of cinematography and editing, created a complex and compelling exploration of human nature and the elusiveness of truth. The film won the Golden Lion at the Venice Film Festival and an Honorary Academy Award, cementing Kurosawa's reputation as a visionary filmmaker.

Following the success of "Rashomon," Kurosawa directed "Ikiru" (1952), a poignant drama about a bureaucrat, played by Takashi Shimura, who, upon learning that he has terminal cancer, searches for meaning in his life by building a playground for children. "Ikiru" is a profound meditation on mortality, purpose, and the human condition, showcasing Kurosawa's ability to blend deep philosophical questions with compelling character studies.

Kurosawa's most famous and influential work is arguably "Seven Samurai" (1954), a grand epic that has left an indelible mark on cinema. The film tells the story of a group of samurai who defend a village from bandits, blending action, drama, and social commentary. "Seven Samurai" is renowned for its meticulous direction, dynamic action sequences, and rich character development. The film's narrative structure, ensemble cast, and themes of honor, sacrifice, and solidarity have influenced countless filmmakers and spawned numerous adaptations, including the Western classic "The Magnificent Seven" (1960).

Throughout the 1950s and 1960s, Kurosawa continued to create a series of critically acclaimed films, often collaborating with the actor Toshiro Mifune, who became his frequent leading man. Their partnership produced some of cinema's most memorable characters and performances. Films like "Throne of Blood" (1957), a samurai adaptation of Shakespeare's "Macbeth," "The Hidden Fortress" (1958), a swashbuckling adventure that inspired George Lucas's "Star Wars," and "Yojimbo" (1961), a tale of a wandering ronin who plays two rival gangs against each other, exemplify Kurosawa's versatility and mastery of storytelling.

"Yojimbo" in particular is notable for its stylistic innovation and narrative cunning. The film's protagonist, played by Mifune, is an antihero whose strategic manipulation of events reflects Kurosawa's interest in complex, morally ambiguous characters. The film's influence can be seen in the works of directors like Sergio Leone, whose "A Fistful of Dollars" (1964) was an unofficial remake, and Quentin Tarantino, who has cited Kurosawa as a major influence.

In 1965, Kurosawa directed "Red Beard," a period drama that marked the end of his collaboration with Mifune. The film, set in a rural clinic in 19th-century Japan, is a humanistic exploration of compassion, suffering, and the struggles of the disenfranchised. "Red Beard" is notable for its meticulous production design, powerful performances, and Kurosawa's profound empathy for his characters. Despite its success, the film's lengthy and demanding production led to a period of professional and personal challenges for Kurosawa.

The late 1960s and 1970s were a difficult time for Kurosawa, as he struggled to secure funding for his projects in an industry that was increasingly moving away from traditional filmmaking. His collaboration with the Soviet Union on "Dersu Uzala" (1975), a poignant tale of friendship and survival in the Siberian wilderness, marked a successful return to form. The film won the Academy Award for Best Foreign Language Film and reaffirmed Kurosawa's international reputation.

Kurosawa's later years saw a remarkable resurgence in his career. "Kagemusha" (1980), a historical epic about a thief who is hired to impersonate a dying warlord, was produced with the support of directors George Lucas and Francis Ford Coppola. The film won the Palme d'Or at the Cannes Film Festival and was a critical and commercial success. This was followed by "Ran" (1985), Kurosawa's adaptation of Shakespeare's "King Lear," set in feudal Japan. "Ran" is considered one of Kurosawa's masterpieces, featuring breathtaking visuals, grand battle scenes, and a tragic exploration of power, betrayal, and madness.

Kurosawa continued to create thought-provoking and visually stunning films into the 1990s. "Dreams" (1990) is a deeply personal film composed of eight vignettes inspired by his own dreams, exploring themes of nature, art, war, and mortality. "Rhapsody in August" (1991) and "Madadayo" (1993), his final film, reflect on themes of memory, aging, and the passage of time, showcasing Kurosawa's enduring humanism and reflective spirit.

Kurosawa's contributions to cinema extend beyond his films. He was a pioneer in the use of deep focus, dynamic compositions, and innovative editing techniques, such as the use of wipe transitions and axial cuts. His meticulous attention to detail, from costume and set design to the use of weather and natural elements to enhance mood and symbolism, set new standards for cinematic craftsmanship. Kurosawa's ability to blend traditional Japanese aesthetics with Western influences created a unique and universal cinematic language that transcends cultural boundaries.

Kurosawa's impact on global cinema is immeasurable. His influence can be seen in the works of directors such as Ingmar Bergman, Federico Fellini, Martin Scorsese, Steven Spielberg, and George Lucas, among many others. His films have inspired numerous remakes, adaptations, and homages, and his techniques and storytelling principles continue to be studied and revered by filmmakers and scholars around the world.

In addition to his technical and artistic achievements, Kurosawa was known for his strong moral vision and humanistic philosophy. His films often explore themes of honor, justice, and the struggle between good and evil, reflecting his belief in the potential for human nobility and redemption. Kurosawa's empathy for his characters, regardless of their flaws or social status, and his ability to portray the complexities of the human condition have made his work timeless and universally resonant.

Akira Kurosawa passed away on September 6, 1998, at the age of 88. His death marked the end of an era in cinema, but his legacy continues to thrive. Kurosawa's films remain essential viewing for anyone interested in the art of filmmaking, and his influence is evident in the works of contemporary directors and the ongoing admiration of audiences worldwide. His ability to craft powerful, visually stunning narratives that explore the depths of the human experience has earned him a place among the greatest filmmakers of all time.

Chapter 32: Hayao Miyazaki

Hayao Miyazaki, born on January 5, 1941, in Tokyo, Japan, is a legendary animator, filmmaker, screenwriter, and co-founder of Studio Ghibli, one of the most acclaimed animation studios in the world. Over his illustrious career, Miyazaki has created a body of work that is renowned for its imaginative storytelling, richly detailed worlds, complex characters, and deep environmental and humanistic themes. His films have transcended cultural boundaries, enchanting audiences of all ages around the globe and earning him a place among the greatest filmmakers of all time.

Miyazaki's early life was marked by the tumultuous period of World War II. His family owned a company that manufactured parts for military aircraft, which gave Miyazaki a close view of the war's impact. These experiences influenced his later work, imbuing it with themes of pacifism and the horrors of conflict. As a child, Miyazaki was an avid reader and a passionate fan of manga and animation. He was particularly inspired by the works of Osamu Tezuka, often considered the "god of manga," and he decided to pursue a career in animation.

Miyazaki began his career in 1963 at Toei Animation, where he worked as an in-between artist. During his time at Toei, he quickly demonstrated his talent and creativity, contributing ideas that went beyond his initial role. He worked on notable projects such as "Doggie March" (1963) and "Gulliver's Travels Beyond the Moon" (1965). It was also at Toei that Miyazaki met Isao Takahata, who would become his lifelong collaborator and co-founder of Studio Ghibli.

One of Miyazaki's early significant contributions was to the animated feature "Hols: Prince of the Sun" (1968), directed by Takahata. Although not a commercial success, the film is considered a landmark in Japanese animation for its complex narrative and thematic depth, qualities that would become hallmarks of Miyazaki's work. He continued to develop his skills and reputation with various projects, including television series like "Heidi, Girl of the Alps" (1974) and "Future Boy Conan" (1978), where he served as a director and storyboard artist.

Miyazaki's breakthrough came with the creation of his first feature film as a director, "The Castle of Cagliostro" (1979), a part of the popular "Lupin III" franchise. The film showcased Miyazaki's distinctive style, blending action, adventure, and humor with intricate plotting and compelling characters. While it did not achieve significant box office success, it was critically acclaimed and demonstrated Miyazaki's potential as a filmmaker.

In 1984, Miyazaki released "Nausicaä of the Valley of the Wind," a film based on his own manga series. "Nausicaä" is set in a post-apocalyptic world where humanity struggles to survive amidst toxic jungles and giant insects. The film's protagonist, Princess Nausicaä, embodies many of Miyazaki's recurring themes: a strong female character who loves nature, seeks peace, and fights against destructive forces. "Nausicaä" was a critical and commercial success, establishing Miyazaki as a leading figure in Japanese animation and paving the way for the creation of Studio Ghibli.

In 1985, Miyazaki co-founded Studio Ghibli with Isao Takahata and producer Toshio Suzuki. The studio quickly became known for its high-quality animation and compelling storytelling. The first film produced by Studio Ghibli was "Laputa: Castle in the Sky" (1986), a fantastical adventure about a boy and girl searching for a legendary floating island. The film was a success and further solidified Miyazaki's reputation.

One of Miyazaki's most beloved films is "My Neighbor Totoro" (1988), which tells the story of two young sisters who encounter magical creatures in the countryside while their mother is hospitalized. "Totoro" is a gentle, heartwarming film that captures the wonder of childhood and the beauty of nature. The character of Totoro has since become an iconic symbol of Studio Ghibli and Japanese pop culture.

Miyazaki continued to create a series of critically acclaimed films throughout the 1990s. "Kiki's Delivery Service" (1989) follows a young witch who starts her own delivery service in a new town, exploring themes of independence and self-discovery. "Porco Rosso" (1992) is a unique tale of a World War I fighter pilot who has been transformed into a pig, blending aerial adventure with deeper reflections on identity and the scars of war.

In 1997, Miyazaki released "Princess Mononoke," a landmark film that explored the conflict between industrialization and nature. Set in a mythical past, the film follows the journey of Ashitaka, a young prince cursed by a demon, and San, a girl raised by wolves, as they navigate a world torn by human and natural forces. "Princess Mononoke" was a massive success in Japan and marked Miyazaki's breakthrough in the international market, receiving widespread acclaim for its complex characters, stunning visuals, and powerful environmental message.

Miyazaki's next film, "Spirited Away" (2001), became his most celebrated work. The film tells the story of Chihiro, a young girl who becomes trapped in a mysterious and magical bathhouse run by spirits and must find a way to rescue her parents and return to the human world. "Spirited Away" is a rich tapestry of imagination, filled with memorable characters and intricate details. It won numerous awards, including the Academy Award for Best Animated Feature, and is often cited as one of the greatest animated films ever made.

Following "Spirited Away," Miyazaki continued to create films that showcased his artistic vision and storytelling prowess. "Howl's Moving Castle" (2004), based on the novel by Diana Wynne Jones, is a fantastical tale about a young woman cursed by a witch and her adventures with a mysterious wizard. The film explores themes of love, war, and personal transformation, and was praised for its imaginative world-building and emotional depth.

In 2008, Miyazaki directed "Ponyo," a whimsical and visually stunning film about a young boy who befriends a goldfish princess who longs to become human. Inspired by Hans Christian Andersen's "The Little Mermaid," "Ponyo" is a joyful celebration of childhood and the natural world, filled with vibrant colors and playful imagery.

After announcing his retirement several times, Miyazaki returned to direct "The Wind Rises" (2013), a more somber and reflective film that tells the fictionalized story of Jiro Horikoshi, the designer of the Mitsubishi A6M Zero fighter plane used in World War II. The film explores the tension between artistic aspiration and the moral implications of one's work, and is a poignant meditation on the beauty and tragedy of human endeavor.

Miyazaki's films are characterized by their lush, hand-drawn animation, meticulous attention to detail, and rich, multilayered narratives. He often features strong, independent female protagonists, complex antagonists, and a deep reverence for nature. His storytelling blends elements of fantasy, folklore, and everyday life, creating worlds that feel both fantastical and grounded in reality. Miyazaki's work is also noted for its moral ambiguity, eschewing clear-cut heroes and villains in favor of nuanced characters with their own motivations and flaws.

In addition to his filmmaking, Miyazaki is known for his dedication to environmental and social issues. His films frequently address the consequences of environmental degradation, the dangers of unchecked industrialization, and the importance of living in harmony with nature. Miyazaki's commitment to these themes is reflected in his personal life; he is an advocate for environmental conservation and has supported various ecological initiatives.

Miyazaki's impact on the world of animation and film is profound. He has inspired countless animators, filmmakers, and storytellers with his unique vision and dedication to his craft. His influence can be seen in the works of contemporary directors such as Guillermo del Toro, Wes Anderson, and Pixar's John Lasseter, who have cited Miyazaki as a major inspiration.

Despite his immense success, Miyazaki remains humble and dedicated to his work. He is known for his meticulous approach to animation, often personally overseeing every aspect of production and insisting on hand-drawn techniques even as the industry shifts towards digital animation. His commitment to quality and his passion for storytelling have set a high standard for animation and have earned him a devoted following worldwide.

In 2016, Miyazaki came out of retirement once again to work on a new feature film, "How Do You Live?", inspired by the 1937 novel of the same name by Yoshino Genzaburo. This project reflects Miyazaki's enduring commitment to his art and his desire to continue creating stories that resonate with audiences. The anticipation surrounding the film speaks to Miyazaki's lasting impact and the excitement that his work continues to generate.

Hayao Miyazaki's legacy is one of unparalleled creativity, compassion, and artistic integrity. His films have touched the hearts of millions, offering a unique blend of entertainment and profound reflection on the human condition. As a master storyteller and a pioneer in the world of animation, Miyazaki has not only elevated the medium but also enriched the lives of those who have experienced the magic of his films. His contributions to cinema will be cherished and celebrated for generations to come, ensuring that his vision and values continue to inspire and captivate audiences around the world.

Chapter 33: Walt Disney

Walt Disney, a name synonymous with creativity and imagination, was born on December 5, 1901, in Chicago, Illinois. His early life was marked by a love for drawing and storytelling, which would later form the foundation of his legendary career. As a child, Disney moved to Marceline, Missouri, where he developed a keen interest in art. Encouraged by his parents, he began to draw, sell sketches to neighbors, and soon enrolled in art classes. These formative years were crucial in shaping his artistic skills and entrepreneurial spirit.

In 1919, Disney moved to Kansas City, where he began his career as an illustrator. He worked for a commercial art studio, creating advertisements for newspapers, magazines, and movie theaters. This job was pivotal, providing him with the experience and inspiration to venture into animation. Alongside his friend Ub Iwerks, Disney experimented with animation, eventually creating the Laugh-O-Gram Studio. Though the studio faced financial difficulties and went bankrupt, it served as a learning experience that honed Disney's creative and business acumen.

Undeterred by this setback, Disney moved to Hollywood in 1923, where he established the Disney Brothers Studio with his brother Roy. The duo created a series of successful cartoons, leading to the birth of a beloved character, Oswald the Lucky Rabbit. However, in 1928, Disney lost the rights to Oswald, a devastating blow that turned out to be a blessing in disguise. This loss spurred Disney to create a character that would become an icon in popular culture: Mickey Mouse. The first sound-synchronized cartoon featuring Mickey, "Steamboat Willie," debuted in 1928, revolutionizing the animation industry. Mickey's success catapulted Disney to fame, establishing him as a pioneer in the field.

Disney's innovation didn't stop with Mickey Mouse. He continually pushed the boundaries of animation, producing the first full-length animated feature film, "Snow White and the Seven Dwarfs," in 1937. This project was a massive risk, both financially and artistically, but it paid off immensely, earning unprecedented box office success and critical acclaim. "Snow White" set the standard for future animated films, showcasing Disney's visionary approach and commitment to quality storytelling.

Throughout the 1940s and 1950s, Disney expanded his studio's repertoire with a series of successful animated films, including "Pinocchio," "Fantasia," "Dumbo," and "Bambi." Each film demonstrated his dedication to innovation, employing groundbreaking techniques in animation, sound, and storytelling. Disney's ability to blend art with technology created a new cinematic experience, captivating audiences worldwide.

In addition to his work in animation, Disney ventured into live-action films and television. He produced popular shows like "The Mickey Mouse Club" and "The Wonderful World of Disney," which further solidified his influence in entertainment. His studio also produced iconic live-action films such as "Mary Poppins," blending live action and animation in a way that was revolutionary for its time.

One of Disney's most ambitious projects was the creation of Disneyland, a theme park that opened in 1955 in Anaheim, California. Disneyland was a realization of Disney's dream to create a place where families could experience the magic of his films firsthand. The park's success led to the development of other theme parks, including Walt Disney World in Florida, which opened in 1971. These parks became global symbols of imagination and fun, attracting millions of visitors annually.

Disney's creative vision extended beyond entertainment. He was deeply involved in the planning and development of EPCOT (Experimental Prototype Community of Tomorrow), a utopian city designed to showcase the latest advancements in technology and urban living. Although Disney passed away in 1966 before seeing EPCOT completed, his vision for a better future continues to inspire urban planning and innovation.

Walt Disney's legacy is immense and multifaceted. He received numerous accolades throughout his career, including 22 Academy Awards and four honorary Oscars, making him one of the most awarded individuals in the history of the Academy. His influence extends beyond film and theme parks; he shaped the way stories are told and experienced, blending fantasy with reality in a way that resonates across generations.

Disney's creative genius lay not only in his artistic talent but also in his ability to foresee and shape the future of entertainment. He understood the power of storytelling and its ability to evoke emotions, connect people, and create lasting memories. His relentless pursuit of excellence and innovation set a benchmark in the industry, inspiring countless artists, filmmakers, and entrepreneurs.

The impact of Walt Disney's work is evident in the enduring popularity of his creations. Characters like Mickey Mouse, Donald Duck, and Goofy remain beloved icons, while films like "The Lion King," "Beauty and the Beast," and "Frozen" continue to enchant new audiences. Disney's influence extends to the broader cultural landscape, shaping the way we understand and engage with media and entertainment.

Disney's personal philosophy, encapsulated in his famous quote, "If you can dream it, you can do it," reflects his belief in the power of dreams and determination. This ethos drove him to overcome numerous challenges and setbacks, transforming his visions into reality. His story is one of resilience, creativity, and unyielding optimism, serving as a testament to what can be achieved with imagination and hard work.

The company Walt Disney founded continues to thrive, expanding into new realms such as streaming services, acquisitions of major franchises like Marvel and Star Wars, and innovative technological advancements in filmmaking. The Disney brand represents a blend of tradition and innovation, maintaining its foundational values while adapting to the changing landscape of entertainment.

Chapter 34: Oprah Winfrey

Oprah Winfrey, an emblematic figure in American media and culture, was born on January 29, 1954, in Kosciusko, Mississippi. Her early life was marked by poverty and hardship, living with her grandmother on a farm. Despite the challenges, her grandmother instilled in her a love for reading, which became a foundation for her future success. Winfrey's natural talent for oratory was evident early on, and she would often recite Bible verses in church, earning praise for her articulate and expressive delivery.

At the age of six, Winfrey moved to Milwaukee, Wisconsin, to live with her mother, Vernita Lee. Her childhood continued to be tumultuous, characterized by episodes of abuse and instability. However, her academic prowess shone through, and she was later sent to live with her father, Vernon Winfrey, in Nashville, Tennessee. Under his strict guidance, she thrived academically, joining the drama club and competing in oratory contests. She earned a full scholarship to Tennessee State University, where she studied communications.

Winfrey's career in media began while she was still in high school, working part-time as a news reader at a local black radio station. Her passion and talent for broadcasting quickly became apparent, and she was soon hired by a local television station as the youngest and first black female news anchor. Despite initial struggles with the rigid format of news reporting, she found her calling in more personal and human-centered storytelling.

In 1984, Winfrey relocated to Chicago to host "AM Chicago," a low-rated morning talk show. Her empathetic, candid, and warm style resonated with viewers, transforming the show into a massive hit. Within months, it was renamed "The Oprah Winfrey Show," and syndicated nationally by 1986. The show, focusing on personal stories, self-improvement, and social issues, set a new standard in daytime television, blending entertainment with deep, meaningful content.

Winfrey's ability to connect with her audience on a personal level was unparalleled, creating a sense of intimacy and trust that made her a beloved figure.

Winfrey's influence extended far beyond her talk show. She utilized her platform to address pressing social issues, including racism, sexism, and mental health, often sharing her own experiences to foster understanding and empathy. Her book club, launched in 1996, had a profound impact on the publishing industry, with her selected titles often becoming bestsellers. This initiative not only promoted reading but also brought diverse voices and stories to a broader audience.

Winfrey's entrepreneurial spirit led her to establish Harpo Productions in 1988, taking control of her brand and expanding her influence in the entertainment industry. Through Harpo, she produced films, television shows, and later, the Oprah Winfrey Network (OWN). Her production company was behind critically acclaimed projects such as "The Color Purple," "Beloved," and the Academy Award-winning film "Precious." OWN, launched in 2011, further solidified her status as a media mogul, offering a range of programming focused on empowerment, spirituality, and self-improvement.

One of Winfrey's most significant contributions is her philanthropic work. She established the Oprah Winfrey Foundation and the Oprah Winfrey Operating Foundation, supporting education, health care, and advocacy for women and children. In 2007, she opened the Oprah Winfrey Leadership Academy for Girls in South Africa, providing quality education and leadership training to disadvantaged girls. Her charitable efforts have had a tangible impact on countless lives, reflecting her commitment to using her wealth and influence for the greater good.

In addition to her professional achievements, Winfrey's personal life has also been a source of inspiration. Her candid discussions about her struggles with weight, relationships, and self-esteem resonated with millions, breaking down stigmas and encouraging others to pursue personal growth. Her long-term partnership with Stedman Graham and her close friendship with Gayle King have been well-documented, showcasing her value for deep, meaningful relationships.

Winfrey's impact on popular culture is immeasurable. She popularized the concept of "confessional" media, where personal experiences are shared openly to promote healing and understanding. Her endorsement power, often referred to as "The Oprah Effect," has the ability to transform products, books, and individuals into overnight successes. Her influence extends to politics as well; her endorsement of Barack Obama in the 2008 presidential election was considered a significant factor in his victory.

Throughout her career, Winfrey has received numerous accolades, including the Presidential Medal of Freedom in 2013, honorary degrees from prestigious universities, and multiple Emmy Awards. Her work has earned her a place in the National Women's Hall of Fame and a star on the Hollywood Walk of Fame. Her legacy is a testament to her extraordinary ability to connect with people, inspire change, and uplift those around her.

Winfrey's foray into different media formats has also been notable. She ventured into the digital space with Oprah.com, providing a platform for self-help content, community engagement, and her extensive archive of interviews and shows. Her podcast, "Oprah's SuperSoul Conversations," features in-depth discussions with thought leaders, authors, and spiritual teachers, continuing her mission to inspire and enlighten.

In recent years, Winfrey has continued to evolve her brand and impact. She signed a multi-year content partnership with Apple, producing original programs that include documentaries, interviews, and book clubs, accessible to a global audience. This collaboration has expanded her reach even further, adapting to the changing media landscape and continuing to influence and inspire new generations.

Winfrey's journey from a troubled childhood to becoming one of the most powerful and influential women in the world is a remarkable testament to her resilience, vision, and unwavering commitment to her values. Her life story embodies the principles of hard work, perseverance, and the transformative power of education and empathy. She has not only shaped the media landscape but also contributed significantly to social change, philanthropy, and personal empowerment.

Chapter 35: Beyoncé Knowles

Beyoncé Knowles, a multifaceted artist and cultural icon, was born on September 4, 1981, in Houston, Texas. From an early age, her talent for performing was evident. Encouraged by her parents, Mathew and Tina Knowles, Beyoncé pursued her passion for music and dance with unwavering dedication. Her father, Mathew, played a pivotal role in her early career, managing and guiding her path to stardom. Beyoncé's journey began with participation in local talent shows and competitions, where she often emerged victorious due to her exceptional singing and dancing abilities.

Her first major breakthrough came as a member of the girl group Destiny's Child, which she formed with childhood friends Kelly Rowland and LaTavia Roberson. The group underwent several lineup changes before stabilizing with Beyoncé, Kelly Rowland, and Michelle Williams. Managed by Mathew Knowles, Destiny's Child signed with Columbia Records and released their debut album in 1998. The group achieved massive success with hits like "No, No, No" and "Bills, Bills, Bills." Their sophomore album, "The Writing's on the Wall," solidified their place in the music industry, featuring chart-topping singles like "Say My Name" and "Jumpin', Jumpin'."

Destiny's Child became one of the best-selling girl groups of all time, known for their tight harmonies, empowering lyrics, and dynamic performances. Beyoncé's role as the lead singer highlighted her powerful voice and commanding stage presence. The group's success laid the foundation for her solo career, showcasing her ability to captivate audiences and dominate the charts.

In 2003, Beyoncé released her debut solo album, "Dangerously in Love," which was both a critical and commercial triumph. The album featured hit singles such as "Crazy in Love" and "Baby Boy," and earned her five Grammy Awards. Her blend of R&B, pop, and hip-hop, combined with her distinctive voice and charismatic performances, set her apart as a solo artist. The album's success marked the beginning of Beyoncé's transformation into a global superstar.

Beyoncé's subsequent albums further established her as a dominant force in the music industry. "B'Day" (2006) continued her streak of hits with songs like "Déjà Vu" and "Irreplaceable." Her evolution as an artist was evident in the diverse musical styles and themes she explored, from love and heartbreak to female empowerment and social justice. Each album showcased her growth as a singer, songwriter, and producer, reflecting her commitment to artistic excellence.

In 2008, Beyoncé released "I Am... Sasha Fierce," a double album that introduced her alter ego, Sasha Fierce. This project highlighted her versatility, with one disc featuring ballads and introspective tracks, and the other showcasing up-tempo, dance-oriented songs. Hits like "Single Ladies (Put a Ring on It)" and "Halo" became anthems, cementing her status as a pop culture icon. The album's success was accompanied by a world tour that demonstrated her unparalleled ability to connect with audiences through electrifying performances.

Beyond her music career, Beyoncé has made significant contributions to film and acting. She starred in several movies, including "Dreamgirls" (2006), for which she received critical acclaim for her portrayal of Deena Jones. Her role in the film showcased her acting prowess and further expanded her influence in the entertainment industry. She also lent her voice to the character of Nala in Disney's 2019 live-action adaptation of "The Lion King," contributing to the film's success with her powerful vocals.

Beyoncé's impact extends beyond entertainment. She is a vocal advocate for social justice, using her platform to address issues such as racial inequality, gender discrimination, and police brutality. Her 2016 album "Lemonade" is a testament to her commitment to these causes. The album, accompanied by a visually stunning film, explored themes of infidelity, forgiveness, and black womanhood. "Lemonade" was hailed as a cultural and artistic milestone, earning widespread acclaim for its bold storytelling and innovative approach.

In 2018, Beyoncé made history as the first black woman to headline the Coachella Valley Music and Arts Festival. Her performance, dubbed "Beychella," celebrated African American culture and history, featuring a marching band, step dancers, and tributes to historically black colleges and universities (HBCUs). The performance was a tour de force, highlighting her dedication to honoring her heritage and inspiring future generations. The live album "Homecoming," released in 2019, captured this iconic performance, further solidifying her legacy.

Beyoncé's entrepreneurial spirit is evident in her ventures beyond music. She co-founded the fashion line House of Deréon with her mother and launched her own athletic wear brand, Ivy Park. Her business acumen and commitment to empowering others are reflected in her various partnerships and endorsements, from fashion to technology. Her influence extends to philanthropy as well; she established the BeyGOOD initiative, supporting causes such as disaster relief, education, and global poverty.

Her personal life, particularly her marriage to rapper and businessman Jay-Z, has also been a subject of public fascination. Together, they are one of the most influential power couples in the entertainment industry. Their collaborative projects, including the album "Everything Is Love" (2018) released under the name The Carters, have garnered critical acclaim and commercial success. Their relationship, marked by both challenges and triumphs, has been candidly documented in their music, offering a glimpse into their lives and their commitment to each other and their family.

Beyoncé's influence is further underscored by her use of visual storytelling. Her 2013 self-titled album introduced the concept of a visual album, with music videos for each song, released without prior announcement. This innovative approach redefined the album release strategy and demonstrated her ability to shape industry trends. She continued this trend with "Lemonade" and the visual album "Black Is King" (2020), which celebrated African culture and heritage, further showcasing her artistic vision and cultural impact.

Her accolades and achievements are numerous. She has won 28 Grammy Awards, making her one of the most awarded artists in Grammy history. Her influence has been recognized with numerous honors, including being named one of Time magazine's most influential people multiple times. Beyoncé's impact on fashion, music, and culture is profound, shaping trends and inspiring countless artists and fans worldwide.

Beyoncé's commitment to empowerment and representation is evident in her dedication to uplifting marginalized voices. She has been a strong advocate for women's rights and equality, both through her music and her philanthropic efforts. Her work with organizations like Chime for Change and the #BeyGood initiative demonstrates her commitment to creating positive change and addressing systemic issues affecting women and girls globally.

In addition to her professional and philanthropic accomplishments, Beyoncé's role as a mother has also influenced her work and public persona. She and Jay-Z have three children: Blue Ivy, and twins Rumi and Sir. Motherhood has added depth to her artistry, as seen in songs like "Blue" and her dedication to creating a better world for future generations. Her emphasis on family and legacy underscores her multifaceted identity as an artist, entrepreneur, advocate, and mother.

Chapter 36: David Bowie

David Bowie, born David Robert Jones on January 8, 1947, in Brixton, London, is a figure whose influence on music, fashion, and popular culture is immense and enduring. Known for his distinctive voice, innovative music, and constant reinvention, Bowie's career spanned five decades and produced a body of work that has left an indelible mark on the world. From his early life to his final album, Bowie's journey is one of relentless creativity and transformation.

Bowie's early years were marked by a fascination with music and performance. He was introduced to rock and roll through the records his father brought home, and by the age of 13, he was playing the saxophone. His early influences included Little Richard, Elvis Presley, and the jazz greats of the time. Bowie attended Bromley Technical High School, where he studied art, music, and design, showing an early interest in the theatrical aspects of performance. His first band, The Konrads, was formed while he was still in school, but it was his solo work that would eventually propel him to stardom.

In the 1960s, Bowie began experimenting with various musical styles and personas. His early attempts to break into the music industry were met with limited success, but he gained attention with his 1969 single "Space Oddity." The song, inspired by Stanley Kubrick's film "2001: A Space Odyssey," told the story of Major Tom, an astronaut who becomes lost in space. "Space Oddity" was a breakthrough hit, reaching the top five in the UK charts and establishing Bowie as a unique voice in rock music.

The early 1970s marked the beginning of Bowie's most iconic and influential period. Embracing the glam rock movement, he created the alter ego Ziggy Stardust, an androgynous rock star from another planet. The album "The Rise and Fall of Ziggy Stardust and the Spiders from Mars" (1972) was a concept album that chronicled the rise and fall of this fictional character. Ziggy Stardust's flamboyant costumes, theatrical performances, and bold exploration of gender and identity challenged conventional norms and captivated audiences. Songs like "Starman" and "Suffragette City" became anthems, and the album is now considered one of the greatest in rock history.

Following the success of Ziggy Stardust, Bowie continued to reinvent himself with each new project. His 1973 album "Aladdin Sane" featured a more polished rock sound and hits like "The Jean Genie" and "Drive-In Saturday." Bowie's fascination with soul and R&B led to the creation of the Thin White Duke persona in the mid-1970s. This period produced the album "Young Americans" (1975), which included the hit single "Fame," co-written with John Lennon. The song became Bowie's first number-one hit in the United States.

In 1976, Bowie released "Station to Station," an album that marked a transition from his soul influences to a more experimental sound. During this time, he moved to Berlin to escape the excesses of rock stardom and to seek artistic rejuvenation. The Berlin Trilogy, consisting of the albums "Low" (1977), "Heroes" (1977), and "Lodger" (1979), was a collaboration with musician Brian Eno. These albums incorporated elements of electronic music, ambient soundscapes, and avant-garde experimentation, significantly influencing the post-punk and new wave movements. "Heroes," the title track from the second album in the trilogy, remains one of Bowie's most enduring and inspirational songs.

The 1980s saw Bowie achieving commercial success with a more mainstream pop sound. His 1983 album "Let's Dance," produced by Nile Rodgers, featured hits like "China Girl," "Modern Love," and the title track "Let's Dance." The album's polished production and danceable beats brought Bowie a new audience and cemented his status as a global superstar. He continued to experiment with different musical styles throughout the decade, collaborating with artists like Queen on the hit single "Under Pressure" and exploring jazz influences on the album "Tonight" (1984).

Bowie's career in the 1990s and 2000s was marked by continued experimentation and reinvention. He embraced industrial rock and electronic music on the album "Outside" (1995), a collaboration with Brian Eno that explored themes of art, crime, and dystopia. The album "Earthling" (1997) incorporated elements of drum and bass and techno, reflecting Bowie's interest in contemporary music trends. Throughout this period, Bowie remained a prolific and influential artist, consistently pushing the boundaries of his sound and persona.

In addition to his music, Bowie had a successful career as an actor. His notable film roles included the alien Thomas Jerome Newton in "The Man Who Fell to Earth" (1976), the Goblin King in "Labyrinth" (1986), and Nikola Tesla in "The Prestige" (2006). Bowie's performances were characterized by his enigmatic presence and ability to embody a wide range of characters, further showcasing his versatility and creativity.

Bowie's final years were marked by a return to music after a decade-long hiatus. In 2013, he released "The Next Day," his first album in ten years. The album was met with critical acclaim and commercial success, reaffirming Bowie's status as a vital and relevant artist. His final album, "Blackstar," was released on January 8, 2016, his 69th birthday. The album was a bold and experimental work that incorporated elements of jazz and avant-garde music. Bowie's death from liver cancer just two days after the release of "Blackstar" added a poignant dimension to the album, with many interpreting it as a parting gift and a reflection on mortality.

David Bowie's legacy is one of perpetual change and innovation. He continually challenged himself and his audience, never content to repeat past successes or rest on his laurels. His ability to anticipate and influence cultural shifts made him a guiding light in the ever-evolving landscape of music and fashion. Bowie's impact can be seen in the work of countless artists who have drawn inspiration from his fearless creativity and willingness to defy conventions.

Bowie's influence extended beyond his music and performances. He was a fashion icon whose style evolved with each new persona he created. From the androgynous glam of Ziggy Stardust to the slick sophistication of the Thin White Duke, Bowie's fashion choices were as innovative and impactful as his music. His willingness to blur the lines between gender and genre challenged societal norms and inspired a generation of designers, musicians, and fans to embrace their individuality and creativity.

In his personal life, Bowie was known for his intelligence, wit, and curiosity. He was an avid reader and collector of art, with a keen interest in the works of modern and contemporary artists. His marriage to supermodel Iman in 1992 was a testament to his enduring search for meaningful connection and partnership. The couple remained together until his death, and their relationship was characterized by mutual respect, love, and admiration.

Bowie's philanthropic efforts were also notable. He supported numerous charitable causes throughout his life, including efforts to combat HIV/AIDS, promote education, and support the arts. His legacy as a humanitarian is reflected in the many tributes and charitable endeavors inspired by his life and work.

Chapter 37: Bob Dylan

Bob Dylan, born Robert Allen Zimmerman on May 24, 1941, in Duluth, Minnesota, is a figure whose influence on music, literature, and culture is profound and far-reaching. His career, which spans over six decades, has been marked by a continuous evolution of style and a relentless quest for artistic expression. Dylan is celebrated not only for his groundbreaking contributions to music but also for his impact as a poet, a cultural icon, and a voice of social and political change.

Dylan's early years were shaped by a deep love for music. Growing up in the mining town of Hibbing, Minnesota, he was exposed to a variety of musical genres, including folk, country, blues, and rock and roll. He was particularly influenced by the music of Woody Guthrie, whose socially conscious folk songs resonated with him deeply. Dylan's admiration for Guthrie's work would later inspire his own approach to songwriting and his commitment to addressing social issues through music.

In 1959, Dylan moved to Minneapolis to attend the University of Minnesota, but he soon dropped out to pursue a career in music. He began performing in local coffeehouses and quickly gained a reputation for his unique voice and compelling performances. In 1961, Dylan moved to New York City, where he immersed himself in the burgeoning folk music scene in Greenwich Village. It was here that he met his idol, Woody Guthrie, who was hospitalized at the time. Dylan's visits to Guthrie and his immersion in the folk community were pivotal experiences that influenced his early work.

Dylan's self-titled debut album, released in 1962, consisted primarily of traditional folk songs and a few original compositions. Although the album did not achieve commercial success, it showcased Dylan's distinctive voice and his ability to reinterpret traditional material. His breakthrough came with his second album, "The Freewheelin' Bob Dylan" (1963), which featured a collection of original songs that established him as a major voice in the folk revival movement. Songs like "Blowin' in the Wind" and "A Hard Rain's A-Gonna Fall" addressed issues of civil rights, war, and social justice, resonating deeply with the era's growing sense of activism and protest.

"The Times They Are a-Changin'" (1964) continued to build on Dylan's reputation as a prophetic voice of his generation. The title track became an anthem for the social and political upheaval of the 1960s, capturing the spirit of change and resistance that defined the era. Dylan's songwriting during this period was characterized by its lyrical depth, poetic imagery, and incisive social commentary. His ability to articulate the hopes and frustrations of a generation made him a central figure in the cultural landscape of the time.

As Dylan's fame grew, he began to explore new musical directions. In 1965, he released "Bringing It All Back Home," an album that marked a significant departure from his folk roots. The album featured a blend of acoustic and electric songs, signaling Dylan's transition to rock music. The release of "Highway 61 Revisited" later that year, with its iconic single "Like a Rolling Stone," solidified Dylan's status as a pioneering force in rock music. "Like a Rolling Stone," with its cutting lyrics and innovative sound, is widely regarded as one of the greatest rock songs of all time.

Dylan's decision to go electric was controversial, sparking backlash from some of his folk purist fans. This tension came to a head at the Newport Folk Festival in 1965, where Dylan's electric performance was met with a mix of boos and cheers. Despite the controversy, Dylan's electric period produced some of his most influential work, including the critically acclaimed albums "Blonde on Blonde" (1966) and "John Wesley Harding" (1967). These albums showcased his ability to blend rock, folk, blues, and country influences into a unique and innovative sound.

In the late 1960s, Dylan retreated from the public eye following a motorcycle accident in 1966. During this period of seclusion, he recorded the informal sessions that would later be released as "The Basement Tapes" with The Band. The music from these sessions reflected a return to a more stripped-down, roots-oriented sound. Dylan's next official release, "Nashville Skyline" (1969), further explored his interest in country music, featuring collaborations with Johnny Cash and showcasing a gentler, more melodic style.

The 1970s saw Dylan continuing to evolve as an artist, exploring different genres and themes. "Blood on the Tracks" (1975), often considered one of his greatest albums, delved into deeply personal themes of love, heartbreak, and redemption. The album's raw emotion and poetic lyricism resonated with listeners, cementing Dylan's reputation as a masterful storyteller. "Desire" (1976), featuring the hit single "Hurricane," addressed issues of injustice and racial discrimination, reflecting Dylan's ongoing commitment to social and political causes.

Dylan's career in the 1980s and 1990s was marked by periods of experimentation and reinvention. He explored religious themes in albums like "Slow Train Coming" (1979) and "Saved" (1980), reflecting his conversion to Christianity. This period of spiritual exploration was met with mixed reactions from fans and critics but demonstrated Dylan's willingness to take risks and explore new artistic directions. The 1980s also saw Dylan collaborating with a range of artists and experimenting with different musical styles, including the formation of the supergroup The Traveling Wilburys with George Harrison, Tom Petty, Jeff Lynne, and Roy Orbison.

In the late 1990s and 2000s, Dylan experienced a resurgence in critical and commercial success. His 1997 album "Time Out of Mind" was hailed as a return to form, winning multiple Grammy Awards, including Album of the Year. The album's themes of mortality, loss, and reflection resonated with audiences and critics alike, marking a new chapter in Dylan's illustrious career. Subsequent albums like "Love and Theft" (2001) and "Modern Times" (2006) continued to receive acclaim, showcasing Dylan's enduring relevance and creative vitality.

Beyond his music, Dylan's influence extends to literature, art, and film. His poetic lyrics have been studied and analyzed for their literary qualities, and he was awarded the Nobel Prize in Literature in 2016 for "having created new poetic expressions within the great American song tradition." This recognition highlighted Dylan's impact as a literary figure and his contribution to the art of songwriting. Dylan is also a visual artist, with his paintings and drawings exhibited in galleries around the world. His work as an actor and filmmaker, including his roles in "Pat Garrett and Billy the Kid" (1973) and the experimental film "Renaldo and Clara" (1978), further demonstrates his multifaceted talents.

Dylan's personal life has also been the subject of much fascination and speculation. His relationships, marriages, and family life have often been kept private, adding to his enigmatic persona. Despite his status as a public figure, Dylan has maintained a sense of mystery and independence, often eschewing the trappings of fame and celebrity.

Chapter 38: John Lennon

John Lennon, born on October 9, 1940, in Liverpool, England, is one of the most influential musicians and cultural figures of the 20th century. As a member of The Beatles and a solo artist, Lennon's contributions to music, art, and social activism have left an indelible mark on the world. His life and work were characterized by a relentless pursuit of truth, creativity, and peace, making him a symbol of hope and change for millions.

Lennon's early life was marked by instability and loss. His parents, Julia and Alfred Lennon, separated when he was a toddler, and he was raised by his maternal aunt, Mimi Smith, in the suburb of Woolton. Despite the absence of his parents, Lennon maintained a close relationship with his mother, Julia, who introduced him to music. Julia's untimely death in a car accident when Lennon was 17 was a devastating blow that profoundly influenced his later work.

Lennon's passion for music blossomed during his teenage years. He formed his first band, The Quarrymen, in 1956, drawing inspiration from the burgeoning rock and roll scene. The Quarrymen evolved into The Beatles, with the addition of Paul McCartney, George Harrison, and later, Ringo Starr. The Beatles quickly became a sensation, revolutionizing popular music with their innovative sound and charismatic performances. Their early hits, like "Please Please Me" and "She Loves You," captured the exuberance of youth and the spirit of the 1960s.

Lennon's songwriting partnership with Paul McCartney is one of the most celebrated collaborations in music history. Together, they crafted a series of timeless classics, blending Lennon's introspective, often acerbic lyrics with McCartney's melodic sensibilities. Songs like "A Hard Day's Night," "Help!," and "In My Life" showcased Lennon's ability to infuse pop music with emotional depth and lyrical sophistication. The Beatles' evolving musical experimentation, from the folk-rock of "Rubber Soul" to the psychedelic sounds of "Sgt. Pepper's Lonely Hearts Club Band," reflected Lennon's restless creativity and willingness to push boundaries.

The Beatles' success brought immense fame and pressure, leading Lennon to explore new artistic directions and personal introspection. In the late 1960s, he met avant-garde artist Yoko Ono, who became his muse and partner in both life and art. Their relationship was marked by a shared commitment to peace, love, and experimental art, challenging conventional norms and expectations. Lennon's collaboration with Ono influenced his songwriting, evident in the raw emotional honesty of songs like "Julia" and "Across the Universe."

The dissolution of The Beatles in 1970 marked a turning point in Lennon's career. Freed from the constraints of the band, he embarked on a solo career that allowed him to express his artistic vision more fully. His debut solo album, "John Lennon/Plastic Ono Band" (1970), was a stark, confessional work that addressed his childhood trauma, existential fears, and search for identity. Songs like "Mother" and "God" laid bare Lennon's vulnerabilities, offering a raw, unfiltered glimpse into his psyche.

Lennon's subsequent albums continued to explore themes of love, peace, and social justice. "Imagine" (1971), his most commercially successful solo album, featured the iconic title track, which became an anthem for peace and hope. The song's simple, yet profound lyrics envisioned a world without war, borders, or religious divisions, resonating deeply with audiences worldwide. Other tracks on the album, such as "Jealous Guy" and "How Do You Sleep?," showcased Lennon's ability to blend personal introspection with broader social commentary.

Throughout the 1970s, Lennon remained a vocal advocate for peace and political activism. He and Ono staged "Bed-Ins for Peace," using their celebrity to protest the Vietnam War and promote nonviolent resistance. Lennon's outspoken views on politics and social issues often put him at odds with authorities, leading to his deportation battle with the U.S. government, which sought to expel him due to his anti-war activism and leftist sympathies. Despite these challenges, Lennon continued to use his platform to speak out against injustice and advocate for a more compassionate world.

Lennon's musical output in the 1970s was diverse and experimental. Albums like "Mind Games" (1973) and "Walls and Bridges" (1974) showcased his ability to blend rock, pop, and avant-garde influences, while also reflecting his personal struggles and triumphs. "Double Fantasy" (1980), a collaboration with Ono, marked Lennon's return to music after a five-year hiatus spent focusing on his family. The album, featuring songs like "(Just Like) Starting Over" and "Woman," celebrated his renewed commitment to love and domestic life.

Tragically, Lennon's life was cut short on December 8, 1980, when he was assassinated outside his apartment building in New York City. His death sent shockwaves around the world, and millions mourned the loss of a beloved artist and visionary. Lennon's legacy, however, continues to inspire and resonate with people across generations. His songs, imbued with messages of peace, love, and self-discovery, remain as relevant today as they were during his lifetime.

Lennon's influence extends beyond his music. As a cultural icon, he embodied the spirit of the 1960s counterculture and the quest for social change. His style, wit, and irreverence challenged societal norms and inspired a generation to question authority and embrace individuality. Lennon's activism, whether through music, art, or public demonstrations, underscored his belief in the power of art to effect change and create a better world.

In addition to his artistic and political contributions, Lennon's personal life and relationships have been the subject of extensive analysis and interest. His complex relationship with his first wife, Cynthia, and their son, Julian, his partnership with Yoko Ono, and his later role as a devoted father to Sean Lennon, all reflect the multifaceted nature of his character. Lennon's willingness to confront his flaws and vulnerabilities, both in his music and his life, has endeared him to fans and admirers who see him as a deeply human figure, striving for redemption and understanding.

Lennon's posthumous influence is vast, with numerous tributes, biographical works, and documentaries celebrating his life and legacy. His induction into the Rock and Roll Hall of Fame, both as a member of The Beatles and as a solo artist, underscores his lasting impact on music. Lennon's songs continue to be covered and performed by artists across genres, a testament to their timeless appeal and enduring relevance.

Chapter 39: Paul McCartney

Paul McCartney, born James Paul McCartney on June 18, 1942, in Liverpool, England, is one of the most celebrated and influential musicians in the history of popular music. As a founding member of The Beatles, a successful solo artist, and a member of the band Wings, McCartney's career spans over six decades and is marked by an unparalleled ability to craft memorable melodies, innovative compositions, and timeless lyrics. His contributions to music, along with his enduring impact on culture and his philanthropic efforts, make him a towering figure in the world of entertainment.

McCartney's early life was shaped by a strong musical and familial foundation. His father, Jim McCartney, was a self-taught musician who played the trumpet and piano, instilling in Paul a love for music from a young age. Tragically, McCartney's mother, Mary, a nurse, died of breast cancer when he was just 14 years old. This profound loss had a lasting impact on McCartney, and the emotional depth it brought to his songwriting would later resonate in many of his compositions.

McCartney's musical journey began in earnest when he met John Lennon at a church fete in 1957. Impressed by McCartney's ability to tune a guitar and his knowledge of popular songs, Lennon invited him to join his band, The Quarrymen. This partnership laid the foundation for what would become one of the most legendary songwriting duos in history. The Quarrymen evolved into The Beatles with the addition of George Harrison and later Ringo Starr, and the band quickly rose to global fame in the early 1960s.

As part of The Beatles, McCartney played a crucial role in shaping the band's sound and artistic direction. His melodic bass lines, versatile musicianship, and knack for songwriting complemented Lennon's more raw and edgy style. Together, they created a series of groundbreaking albums that redefined the possibilities of rock music. McCartney's early contributions to The Beatles' catalog include iconic songs like "Love Me Do," "I Saw Her Standing There," and "All My Loving," which showcased his ability to write catchy, upbeat pop songs.

The mid-1960s marked a period of remarkable creative growth for McCartney and The Beatles. Albums like "Rubber Soul" (1965) and "Revolver" (1966) saw the band exploring new musical territories, incorporating elements of folk, classical, and Indian music into their work. McCartney's compositions during this period, such as "Yesterday," "Eleanor Rigby," and "For No One," demonstrated his mastery of melody and his willingness to experiment with different genres and instrumentation. "Yesterday," in particular, became one of the most covered songs in history, highlighting McCartney's ability to create universally appealing music.

"Sgt. Pepper's Lonely Hearts Club Band" (1967) marked a pinnacle of The Beatles' innovative spirit, and McCartney played a central role in its creation. The concept album, which blended rock, orchestral music, and psychedelia, is often hailed as one of the greatest albums of all time. McCartney's contributions, including "When I'm Sixty-Four," "Lovely Rita," and the title track, reflected his versatility and his talent for creating vivid, character-driven songs. The album's release coincided with the "Summer of Love," and its influence extended far beyond music, impacting fashion, art, and popular culture.

Following the release of "Sgt. Pepper," The Beatles continued to push the boundaries of their music with albums like "The Beatles" (commonly known as the "White Album," 1968), "Abbey Road" (1969), and "Let It Be" (1970). McCartney's songwriting during this period was diverse and eclectic, ranging from the hard-rocking "Helter Skelter" to the introspective "Blackbird" and the anthemic "Hey Jude." "Hey Jude," with its extended coda and sing-along chorus, became one of The Beatles' most beloved songs and showcased McCartney's ability to connect with audiences on a deeply emotional level.

The breakup of The Beatles in 1970 marked the end of an era, but McCartney's career was far from over. He embarked on a solo career with the release of his debut solo album, "McCartney" (1970), which featured the hit single "Maybe I'm Amazed." The album's homemade, lo-fi aesthetic reflected McCartney's desire for creative independence and his ability to produce music outside the confines of a band. "Maybe I'm Amazed" remains one of McCartney's most enduring solo songs, praised for its heartfelt lyrics and powerful vocal performance.

In 1971, McCartney formed the band Wings with his wife, Linda McCartney, and guitarist Denny Laine. Wings became one of the most successful bands of the 1970s, producing a string of hit albums and singles. McCartney's work with Wings demonstrated his ability to adapt to changing musical trends while maintaining his distinctive melodic sensibility. Albums like "Band on the Run" (1973), "Venus and Mars" (1975), and "Wings at the Speed of Sound" (1976) were commercial and critical successes, featuring hits like "Band on the Run," "Jet," "Listen to What the Man Said," and "Silly Love Songs."

"Band on the Run," in particular, is often regarded as one of McCartney's finest achievements. The album's title track, with its three-part structure and dynamic shifts, showcased McCartney's compositional prowess and his ability to craft epic, narrative-driven songs. The album's success solidified McCartney's status as a major solo artist and confirmed his ability to thrive outside the shadow of The Beatles.

Throughout the 1980s and 1990s, McCartney continued to explore new musical directions and collaborate with a wide range of artists. His solo albums from this period, such as "Tug of War" (1982) and "Flowers in the Dirt" (1989), featured collaborations with notable musicians like Stevie Wonder and Elvis Costello. McCartney's willingness to experiment with different styles and genres, from synth-pop to classical music, demonstrated his boundless creativity and his refusal to be pigeonholed.

In addition to his work in popular music, McCartney has made significant contributions to classical music. He composed several classical works, including the oratorio "Liverpool Oratorio" (1991) and the orchestral piece "Standing Stone" (1997). These compositions showcased McCartney's versatility as a composer and his ability to create music that transcends genre boundaries. His interest in classical music reflects his lifelong passion for musical exploration and his desire to challenge himself artistically.

McCartney's influence extends beyond his music. As a cultural icon, he has used his platform to advocate for various causes, including animal rights, vegetarianism, and environmental conservation. McCartney has been a vocal supporter of the vegetarian movement since the 1970s, and he co-founded the Meat Free Monday campaign to encourage people to reduce their meat consumption for the sake of the planet. His activism and philanthropy reflect his commitment to making a positive impact on the world and using his fame for the greater good.

In his personal life, McCartney has experienced both triumphs and tragedies. His marriage to Linda McCartney was a partnership of love and creativity, and together they raised four children. Linda's death from breast cancer in 1998 was a devastating loss for McCartney, but he continued to honor her memory through his music and activism. He later married Heather Mills, with whom he has a daughter, Beatrice, and then Nancy Shevell, finding companionship and support in his later years.

McCartney's legacy is one of unparalleled musical achievement and enduring influence. As a member of The Beatles, he helped shape the sound and direction of popular music, leaving an indelible mark on the cultural landscape. His solo career, marked by a relentless pursuit of innovation and artistic growth, has produced a vast and diverse body of work that continues to resonate with audiences around the world. McCartney's ability to connect with people through his music, his dedication to his craft, and his commitment to social and environmental causes make him a beloved and respected figure in the world of entertainment.

In recognition of his contributions to music and culture, McCartney has received numerous accolades, including multiple Grammy Awards, an Academy Award, and a knighthood from Queen Elizabeth II. His induction into the Rock and Roll Hall of Fame, both as a member of The Beatles and as a solo artist, underscores his enduring impact on the music industry. McCartney's songs, whether performed solo or with The Beatles, have become an integral part of the fabric of popular music, influencing countless artists and inspiring generations of musicians and fans.

Chapter 40: Aretha Franklin

Aretha Franklin, often hailed as the "Queen of Soul," was born on March 25, 1942, in Memphis, Tennessee. Her musical journey and immense contributions to soul, R&B, and gospel music have cemented her place as one of the most influential and celebrated artists in the history of American music. With a career that spanned more than six decades, Franklin's powerful voice, emotive delivery, and indomitable spirit made her a cultural icon whose impact extends far beyond music.

Franklin's early life was deeply intertwined with music and spirituality. She was born to Clarence LaVaughn "C.L." Franklin, a prominent Baptist minister, and Barbara Siggers Franklin, a gifted pianist and vocalist. The family moved to Detroit, Michigan, when Aretha was a young child, where her father became the pastor of New Bethel Baptist Church. C.L. Franklin was known for his fiery sermons and charismatic presence, drawing large crowds and earning him the nickname "The Man with the Million-Dollar Voice." He also recorded several albums of his sermons and gospel music, which were widely distributed.

Aretha's mother, Barbara, left the family when Aretha was just six years old, a traumatic event that deeply affected her. Tragically, Barbara died of a heart attack four years later. Despite these early hardships, Franklin found solace and inspiration in music. She began singing in her father's church, where her prodigious talent quickly became evident. Surrounded by gospel music and the influence of church musicians, Franklin honed her vocal skills and developed a powerful, soulful singing style that would become her trademark.

By the age of 14, Franklin had already recorded her first album, "Songs of Faith," which consisted of gospel music. Her performances caught the attention of prominent figures in the music industry, including gospel greats like Mahalia Jackson and Clara Ward, who became her mentors and advocates. Recognizing her potential, C.L.

Franklin began managing her career, helping to arrange her first recording sessions and public appearances.

In 1960, at the age of 18, Franklin decided to pursue a career in secular music and moved to New York City. She signed with Columbia Records, where she worked with producer John Hammond, a key figure in the careers of many legendary artists. Franklin's early recordings at Columbia showcased her versatility, as she explored various genres, including jazz, blues, and pop. Despite her talent and the quality of her work, Franklin's time at Columbia did not yield the commercial success she desired, as the label struggled to find the right direction for her distinctive voice.

In 1966, Franklin made a pivotal move to Atlantic Records, a decision that would transform her career and solidify her status as a soul music legend. Under the guidance of producer Jerry Wexler, Franklin began recording at FAME Studios in Muscle Shoals, Alabama, a renowned studio known for its "Muscle Shoals Sound." It was here that Franklin found her true musical identity, blending gospel intensity with the raw, emotive power of soul and R&B.

Her first single for Atlantic, "I Never Loved a Man (The Way I Love You)," released in 1967, became a massive hit, reaching number one on the R&B charts and breaking into the top ten on the pop charts. The song's success marked the beginning of an extraordinary period of creativity and commercial success for Franklin. That same year, she released the album "I Never Loved a Man the Way I Love You," which included the iconic track "Respect." Originally written and recorded by Otis Redding, Franklin's rendition of "Respect" became a feminist and civil rights anthem, symbolizing empowerment and resilience. Her powerful delivery and the song's unforgettable call-and-response refrain, "R-E-S-P-E-C-T," resonated deeply with audiences, and it remains one of the most enduring and influential songs in popular music history.

Franklin's success continued with a series of critically acclaimed and commercially successful albums throughout the late 1960s and early 1970s. Albums like "Lady Soul" (1968), "Aretha Now" (1968), and "Spirit in the Dark" (1970) produced a string of hits, including "Chain of Fools," "Think," "I Say a Little Prayer," and "Spanish Harlem." Franklin's music during this period was characterized by its emotional depth, vocal virtuosity, and a seamless blend of gospel, soul, and R&B elements. Her ability to convey profound emotion through her voice, coupled with her exceptional interpretive skills, made her a unique and compelling artist.

In addition to her musical achievements, Franklin became a symbol of the civil rights movement. Her music provided a soundtrack for the struggle for racial equality, and her performances at civil rights rallies and benefit concerts underscored her commitment to social justice. Franklin's father, C.L. Franklin, was a close friend of Dr. Martin Luther King Jr., and Aretha herself had a strong connection to the movement. In 1968, she sang at King's funeral, performing a stirring rendition of "Precious Lord, Take My Hand," a gospel song that held deep significance for the civil rights leader.

The 1970s saw Franklin continue to dominate the music scene with her powerful voice and compelling performances. She experimented with different musical styles, including rock, funk, and disco, demonstrating her versatility and adaptability as an artist. Her 1972 album "Young, Gifted and Black" featured socially conscious songs and highlighted her continued relevance in the changing musical landscape. The album earned her a Grammy Award and further solidified her status as a trailblazing artist.

One of Franklin's most significant achievements during the 1970s was her return to gospel music with the live album "Amazing Grace" (1972). Recorded at the New Temple Missionary Baptist Church in Los Angeles, the album captured the raw energy and spiritual fervor of Franklin's gospel roots. "Amazing Grace" became one of the best-selling gospel albums of all time and showcased Franklin's unparalleled ability to connect with audiences on a deeply emotional and spiritual level.

As the music industry evolved in the 1980s and 1990s, Franklin continued to adapt and thrive. She signed with Arista Records in 1980 and collaborated with producer Clive Davis, who helped revitalize her career. The move to Arista resulted in several successful albums, including "Jump to It" (1982) and "Who's Zoomin' Who?" (1985). The latter album featured the hit single "Freeway of Love," which earned Franklin a Grammy Award and reestablished her as a force in contemporary music.

Franklin's ability to stay relevant in the ever-changing music industry was a testament to her talent, resilience, and unwavering dedication to her craft. She continued to release new music and tour extensively, captivating audiences with her powerful voice and commanding stage presence. Her influence extended to a new generation of artists, who admired her artistry and sought to emulate her success.

Throughout her career, Franklin received numerous accolades and honors, recognizing her immense contributions to music and culture. She won a total of 18 Grammy Awards, including the Grammy Lifetime Achievement Award and the Grammy Legend Award. In 1987, she became the first woman to be inducted into the Rock and Roll Hall of Fame, a historic milestone that underscored her pioneering role in the music industry. Franklin also received the Presidential Medal of Freedom in 2005, the highest civilian honor in the United States, in recognition of her impact on American culture and society.

Franklin's personal life, like her professional career, was marked by triumphs and challenges. She faced numerous personal struggles, including turbulent relationships, financial difficulties, and health issues. Despite these obstacles, Franklin's resilience and determination allowed her to persevere and continue creating music that touched the hearts of millions.

In her later years, Franklin remained a beloved and influential figure, performing at significant events such as the inaugurations of Presidents Bill Clinton and Barack Obama. Her performance of "My Country, 'Tis of Thee" at Obama's 2009 inauguration was particularly memorable, showcasing her enduring ability to inspire and uplift audiences with her powerful voice.

Franklin's final years were marked by declining health, but her spirit and passion for music remained undiminished. She announced her retirement from touring in 2017, although she continued to record and perform on special occasions. Franklin's death on August 16, 2018, at the age of 76, was met with an outpouring of grief and tributes from fans, fellow musicians, and world leaders. Her passing marked the end of an era, but her legacy lives on through her timeless music and the profound impact she had on the world.

Chapter 41: Freddie Mercury

Freddie Mercury, born Farrokh Bulsara on September 5, 1946, in Zanzibar (now part of Tanzania), was an extraordinary musician, singer, and songwriter, best known as the frontman of the legendary rock band Queen. His remarkable four-octave vocal range, flamboyant stage presence, and ability to blend various musical genres made him one of the most influential and iconic figures in the history of rock music. Mercury's life and career were characterized by immense creativity, a relentless pursuit of artistic excellence, and a profound impact on popular culture.

Mercury was born to Parsi parents from India, Bomi and Jer Bulsara, who were Zoroastrian by faith. His father worked as a cashier at the British Colonial Office, and the family lived a relatively comfortable life. Mercury's early years were spent in Zanzibar and India, where he attended boarding school at St. Peter's School in Panchgani. It was here that he began to show an interest in music, learning to play the piano and participating in school performances. His classmates and teachers quickly recognized his musical talent, and he even formed a school band called The Hectics.

In 1964, amid political unrest in Zanzibar, the Bulsara family moved to England, settling in the town of Feltham, Middlesex. Mercury enrolled at Isleworth Polytechnic (now West Thames College) and later studied graphic design at Ealing Art College. It was during his time at Ealing that he became immersed in the vibrant London music scene, frequenting clubs and concerts and forming friendships with other aspiring musicians. Mercury's early experiences in London would play a crucial role in shaping his musical aspirations and stylistic sensibilities.

In 1969, Mercury joined a band called Ibex, which later became Wreckage, but the group disbanded shortly thereafter. He then joined the band Sour Milk Sea, which also had a brief existence. Undeterred by these setbacks, Mercury continued to pursue his passion for music with unwavering determination. In 1970, he teamed up with guitarist Brian May and drummer Roger Taylor, who were part of a band called Smile. When Smile's bassist and lead singer Tim Staffell left the band, Mercury stepped in as the new lead vocalist, and bassist John Deacon joined shortly after. The quartet rebranded themselves as Queen, and thus began one of the most remarkable journeys in rock history.

From the outset, Queen set out to distinguish themselves with a unique sound that blended rock, opera, and theatricality. Mercury played a pivotal role in shaping the band's identity, contributing his distinctive voice, songwriting prowess, and visionary ideas. The band's self-titled debut album, released in 1973, showcased their eclectic style and musical virtuosity, but it was their subsequent albums that propelled them to global stardom. Mercury's stage persona, characterized by his flamboyant costumes, dynamic performances, and charismatic presence, captivated audiences and set a new standard for live rock shows.

One of Queen's breakthrough moments came with the release of their third album, "Sheer Heart Attack" (1974), which included the hit single "Killer Queen." The song's success established Queen as a major force in the music industry and showcased Mercury's ability to craft sophisticated, catchy pop-rock songs. However, it was their next album, "A Night at the Opera" (1975), that truly cemented their place in rock history. The album featured the groundbreaking track "Bohemian Rhapsody," an ambitious, multi-part composition that blended rock and opera elements. Mercury's vision and the band's meticulous production resulted in a song that defied convention and became a monumental success.

"Bohemian Rhapsody" topped the UK charts for nine weeks and became a defining moment in Queen's career. The song's elaborate structure, innovative use of multi-tracked vocals, and dramatic shifts in style made it a landmark achievement in rock music. The accompanying music video, directed by Bruce Gowers, was also revolutionary, paving the way for the modern music video era. Mercury's fearless creativity and willingness to push boundaries were key to the song's enduring legacy.

Queen's subsequent albums, including "A Day at the Races" (1976), "News of the World" (1977), and "Jazz" (1978), continued to showcase the band's versatility and Mercury's dynamic range as a vocalist and songwriter. Tracks like "Somebody to Love," "We Are the Champions," and "Don't Stop Me Now" became anthems that resonated with fans worldwide. Mercury's ability to convey deep emotion through his voice, whether it was the vulnerability of "Love of My Life" or the exuberance of "Crazy Little Thing Called Love," made him one of the most compelling performers of his generation.

In addition to his work with Queen, Mercury pursued a successful solo career. His first solo album, "Mr. Bad Guy," released in 1985, featured a mix of disco, pop, and rock elements. While the album received mixed reviews, it showcased Mercury's willingness to explore different musical styles and his continued evolution as an artist. Mercury also collaborated with Spanish opera singer Montserrat Caballé on the album "Barcelona" (1988), which blended opera and rock in a unique and ambitious project. The title track, "Barcelona," became an anthem for the 1992 Summer Olympics and highlighted Mercury's ability to transcend genre boundaries.

One of the most iconic moments in Mercury's career came on July 13, 1985, when Queen performed at the Live Aid concert at Wembley Stadium. Their 20-minute set, which included hits like "Bohemian Rhapsody," "Radio Ga Ga," and "We Are the Champions," is widely regarded as one of the greatest live performances in rock history. Mercury's electrifying stage presence and ability to connect with the audience on a massive scale demonstrated his unparalleled showmanship and solidified Queen's legacy as one of the greatest live bands of all time.

Despite his public persona, Mercury was known to be a private individual who guarded his personal life closely. He was openly gay, but he maintained a discreet personal life, sharing his experiences with a close circle of friends and loved ones. Mercury's longtime partner, Jim Hutton, remained by his side until the end of his life. His relationships and experiences influenced many of his songs, adding layers of depth and authenticity to his music.

In the late 1980s, Mercury was diagnosed with AIDS, a devastating blow that he initially kept private. Despite his declining health, he continued to record and perform with Queen, displaying remarkable courage and dedication. The band's final albums with Mercury, including "The Miracle" (1989) and "Innuendo" (1991), featured some of his most poignant and powerful work. Songs like "These Are the Days of Our Lives" and "The Show Must Go On" reflected his strength and determination in the face of adversity.

Mercury's final public appearance was in 1990, when Queen received the Brit Award for Outstanding Contribution to British Music. By this time, his health had deteriorated significantly, but his spirit and passion for music remained undiminished. On November 23, 1991, Mercury issued a public statement confirming his AIDS diagnosis, and he passed away just 24 hours later, on November 24, 1991, at the age of 45. His death was a profound loss to the music world, but his legacy endures through his timeless music and the impact he had on countless fans and artists.

In the years following his death, Mercury's influence continued to grow. The posthumous release of the album "Made in Heaven" (1995), which featured previously unreleased Queen tracks and new material recorded by the band, served as a testament to Mercury's enduring artistry. The album included the poignant track "Mother Love," the last song Mercury recorded, highlighting his indomitable spirit and dedication to his craft.

Mercury's legacy extends beyond his music. He is remembered as a trailblazer who challenged conventions and broke down barriers, both in his music and his personal life. His flamboyant stage presence, unapologetic individuality, and fearless creativity have inspired generations of musicians and performers. Mercury's influence can be seen in the work of artists across genres, from rock and pop to opera and musical theater.

In recognition of his contributions to music and culture, Mercury has received numerous posthumous honors. He was inducted into the Rock and Roll Hall of Fame with Queen in 2001, and the band's music continues to be celebrated through various tributes, documentaries, and biographical films. The 2018 film "Bohemian Rhapsody," which chronicled Mercury's life and career, brought his story to a new generation of fans and earned widespread acclaim, including four Academy Awards.

Chapter 42: Michael Jackson

Michael Jackson, often hailed as the "King of Pop," was born on August 29, 1958, in Gary, Indiana. He emerged as a global icon and one of the most influential entertainers in the history of music. Jackson's unparalleled talent, innovative approach to music and dance, and his profound impact on popular culture have left an indelible mark on the world. His career, spanning over four decades, saw him evolve from a child prodigy in the Jackson 5 to a solo superstar whose influence extended far beyond the realm of music.

Michael Joseph Jackson was the eighth of ten children in the Jackson family, a working-class African-American family. His father, Joseph Jackson, was a steel mill worker and a strict disciplinarian, while his mother, Katherine Jackson, was a devout Jehovah's Witness. From a young age, Michael demonstrated remarkable musical talent. His father, recognizing his children's potential, formed the Jackson 5, a Motown vocal group that included Michael and his older brothers Jackie, Tito, Jermaine, and Marlon. The group quickly gained popularity with their energetic performances, tight harmonies, and Michael's exceptional singing and dancing abilities.

The Jackson 5's debut single, "I Want You Back," released in 1969, became a number one hit on the Billboard Hot 100 chart, followed by other chart-topping singles such as "ABC," "The Love You Save," and "I'll Be There." Michael, as the lead vocalist, became the focal point of the group, captivating audiences with his charisma and vocal prowess. Despite the immense success of the Jackson 5, Michael harbored ambitions of pursuing a solo career, and in 1971, he released his first solo album, "Got to Be There."

While continuing to perform with the Jackson 5, Michael's solo career began to gain momentum. His 1972 hit single "Ben," a heartfelt ballad about a pet rat, showcased his ability to convey deep emotion through his voice. However, it was his collaboration with producer

Quincy Jones that would propel him to unprecedented heights. The partnership began with the album "Off the Wall" in 1979, which marked a significant turning point in Michael's career. The album's blend of pop, rock, funk, and disco elements, combined with Michael's extraordinary vocal range and innovative production techniques, resulted in a groundbreaking sound that captivated audiences worldwide.

"Off the Wall" produced several hit singles, including "Don't Stop 'Til You Get Enough" and "Rock with You," both of which showcased Michael's signature falsetto and infectious dance rhythms. The album's success established him as a solo artist in his own right and earned him his first Grammy Award. However, Michael's ambition and creativity knew no bounds, and he was determined to push the boundaries of music and performance even further.

In 1982, Michael released "Thriller," an album that would become the best-selling album of all time, with estimated sales of over 66 million copies worldwide. "Thriller" was a monumental achievement, featuring a diverse array of tracks that blended pop, rock, R&B, and funk. The album's success was propelled by its iconic music videos, which revolutionized the medium and set new standards for creativity and storytelling. The video for the title track, "Thriller," directed by John Landis, was a groundbreaking 14-minute short film that combined horror, dance, and music in an unprecedented way. The video's choreography, particularly the zombie dance sequence, became a cultural phenomenon and remains one of the most iconic moments in music video history.

"Thriller" produced a string of hit singles, including "Billie Jean," "Beat It," "Wanna Be Startin' Somethin'," and "Human Nature." "Billie Jean," with its unforgettable bassline and compelling narrative, became one of Michael's signature songs and showcased his ability to blend storytelling with music. The song's performance on the television special "Motown 25: Yesterday, Today, Forever" featured Michael's legendary moonwalk dance move, which became a defining moment in his career and solidified his status as a pop culture icon.

"Beat It," featuring a guitar solo by Eddie Van Halen, was another standout track from "Thriller," merging rock and pop in a way that appealed to a wide audience. The song's anti-gang violence message and its powerful music video further demonstrated Michael's ability to address social issues through his art. The album's success earned Michael eight Grammy Awards, including Album of the Year, and solidified his place as the reigning king of pop music.

Michael's follow-up albums, "Bad" (1987) and "Dangerous" (1991), continued to build on his legacy. "Bad," produced again by Quincy Jones, featured hit singles such as "Bad," "The Way You Make Me Feel," "Man in the Mirror," and "Smooth Criminal." The album showcased Michael's evolving musical style, incorporating more rock and electronic elements while maintaining his signature pop sensibility. The "Bad" world tour became one of the highest-grossing tours of all time, further cementing Michael's status as a global superstar.

"Dangerous," produced by Teddy Riley, marked a departure from Michael's collaboration with Quincy Jones and introduced a new jack swing sound that blended R&B, hip-hop, and electronic music. The album included hits like "Black or White," "Remember the Time," "In the Closet," and "Heal the World." "Black or White," with its powerful message of racial harmony and its groundbreaking morphing visual effects in the music video, became an anthem for unity and tolerance.

Throughout his career, Michael Jackson was known for his philanthropic efforts and his commitment to various social causes. He used his platform to raise awareness and funds for issues such as child welfare, education, and the fight against HIV/AIDS. His 1985 collaboration with Lionel Richie on the charity single "We Are the World," which featured numerous artists and raised millions of dollars for famine relief in Africa, was a testament to his dedication to humanitarian efforts. Michael also founded the Heal the World

Foundation in 1992, aiming to improve the lives of children and address global issues such as poverty and disease.

Michael's influence extended beyond music and philanthropy to fashion and dance. His distinctive style, characterized by military jackets, single gloves, fedora hats, and his signature white socks and black loafers, became iconic and inspired countless artists and fans. His innovative dance moves, including the moonwalk, the robot, and his gravity-defying lean in "Smooth Criminal," revolutionized the art of dance and set new standards for performance.

Despite his immense success, Michael's life was not without controversy and personal struggles. His appearance and changing skin color were the subjects of intense media scrutiny, leading to widespread speculation and rumors. Michael later revealed that he suffered from vitiligo, a condition that causes the loss of skin pigmentation. His personal relationships, including his marriages to Lisa Marie Presley and Debbie Rowe, as well as his role as a father to his three children, were also closely followed by the media.

In the 1990s and 2000s, Michael faced several legal challenges and allegations of child sexual abuse, which significantly impacted his career and public image. He vehemently denied the allegations and was acquitted of all charges in a high-profile trial in 2005. Despite the controversies, his loyal fan base remained devoted to him, and his influence on music and culture continued to endure.

In the years leading up to his death, Michael was preparing for a series of comeback concerts titled "This Is It," which were set to take place at the O2 Arena in London. The concerts were highly anticipated and marked his return to the stage after a long hiatus. However, on June 25, 2009, the world was shocked by the news of Michael Jackson's sudden death at the age of 50. The cause of death was acute propofol and benzodiazepine intoxication, and his personal physician, Dr. Conrad Murray, was later convicted of involuntary manslaughter.

Michael Jackson's death was a profound loss to the music world, but his legacy lives on through his timeless music, innovative performances, and the indelible impact he had on popular culture. His influence can be seen in the work of countless artists across various genres, from pop and R&B to hip-hop and rock. His ability to transcend cultural and generational boundaries, his dedication to social causes, and his unparalleled artistry have solidified his place as one of the greatest entertainers of all time.

In the years following his death, numerous tributes and commemorations have celebrated Michael's life and contributions to music. The 2010 release of the documentary "Michael Jackson's This Is It," which chronicled the rehearsals for his planned comeback concerts, provided an intimate look at his creative process and his enduring passion for performance. The film became a box office success and offered fans a final glimpse of Michael's artistic genius.

Michael's posthumous releases, including the albums "Michael" (2010) and "Xscape" (2014), featured previously unreleased tracks and continued to showcase his innovative approach to music. His influence on contemporary artists remains profound, with many citing him as a major inspiration for their work. Michael's impact on music videos, fashion, and dance continues to be felt, and his pioneering contributions to these fields have left a lasting legacy.

Michael Jackson's induction into the Rock and Roll Hall of Fame as both a member of the Jackson 5 and a solo artist, his numerous Grammy Awards, and his status as one of the best-selling music artists of all time are testaments to his extraordinary talent and enduring legacy. His contributions to music, dance, and popular culture have shaped the landscape of entertainment and continue to inspire new generations of artists and fans.

Chapter 43: Madonna

Madonna, often referred to as the "Queen of Pop," is one of the most iconic and influential figures in the history of popular music and culture. Born Madonna Louise Ciccone on August 16, 1958, in Bay City, Michigan, she rose to prominence in the early 1980s and has since maintained a career that spans more than four decades. Madonna's ability to constantly reinvent herself, push boundaries, and provoke thought has made her a defining force in music, fashion, and societal norms. Her journey from a small-town girl to a global superstar is a testament to her relentless ambition, creativity, and resilience.

Madonna's early life was marked by significant challenges and loss. She was the third of six children in a devout Catholic family. Her mother, also named Madonna, died of breast cancer when she was just five years old, a tragedy that deeply affected her and influenced much of her later work. Her father, Silvio "Tony" Ciccone, later remarried, creating a blended family dynamic that was sometimes strained. Despite these difficulties, Madonna was an excellent student and demonstrated an early interest in performance. She attended St. Frederick's and St. Andrew's Catholic Elementary Schools, followed by West Middle School. Madonna's involvement in cheerleading and theater laid the groundwork for her future in entertainment.

In 1976, Madonna moved to New York City with dreams of becoming a professional dancer. She arrived with little money and worked a variety of jobs to support herself, including waitressing and nude modeling. She studied with the Alvin Ailey American Dance Theater and took classes at the American Dance Center. During this time, she formed several bands, including Breakfast Club and Emmy, which helped her develop her musical skills and stage presence. Her early forays into music were characterized by a raw, punk-inspired energy that would later evolve into the polished pop sound that made her famous.

Madonna's big break came when she signed with Sire Records in 1982. Her debut single, "Everybody," became a hit in the dance clubs, and her self-titled debut album, released in 1983, produced several hits, including "Holiday," "Lucky Star," and "Borderline." These songs showcased her ability to blend catchy pop hooks with danceable rhythms, setting the stage for her future success. Her provocative style and unapologetic attitude quickly set her apart from her contemporaries.

The release of her second album, "Like a Virgin" (1984), catapulted Madonna to superstardom. The title track became a cultural phenomenon, thanks in part to her controversial performance at the inaugural MTV Video Music Awards, where she rolled around on stage in a wedding dress. The album also included hits like "Material Girl" and "Dress You Up," which solidified her image as a bold and sexually confident artist. "Like a Virgin" became her first number-one album on the Billboard 200 chart, and its success marked the beginning of her reign as the Queen of Pop.

Throughout the 1980s, Madonna continued to push the boundaries of music and fashion. Her third album, "True Blue" (1986), showcased her versatility with hits like "Papa Don't Preach," "Open Your Heart," and "Live to Tell." The album's diverse range of styles, from pop to ballads, demonstrated her growth as an artist and songwriter. "Papa Don't Preach," with its narrative about teenage pregnancy, highlighted Madonna's willingness to tackle controversial topics and provoke discussion.

Madonna's impact extended beyond music; she became a fashion icon and trendsetter. Her unique style, characterized by lace gloves, crucifixes, layered jewelry, and bold makeup, influenced a generation of young women. She collaborated with designers like Jean-Paul Gaultier, whose cone bras and corsets became synonymous with her image. Madonna's ability to constantly reinvent her look and persona kept her at the forefront of the fashion world and cemented her status as a cultural icon.

The late 1980s and early 1990s saw Madonna expand her influence into film and other media. She starred in the critically acclaimed film "Desperately Seeking Susan" (1985), which showcased her acting talents and further broadened her appeal. Her role in the film "Evita" (1996), for which she won a Golden Globe Award for Best Actress, demonstrated her versatility and ability to tackle more serious, dramatic roles. However, her forays into acting were not always well-received; films like "Shanghai Surprise" (1986) and "Swept Away" (2002) were critical and commercial failures. Despite these setbacks, Madonna's resilience and determination allowed her to continue pursuing her passion for acting.

Madonna's 1989 album "Like a Prayer" marked a significant turning point in her career. The album's title track, with its controversial music video featuring religious imagery and themes of race and sexuality, sparked widespread debate and was condemned by the Vatican. Despite—or perhaps because of—the controversy, the song became a massive hit and is considered one of her greatest works. The album also included hits like "Express Yourself," "Cherish," and "Oh Father," showcasing Madonna's ability to blend personal storytelling with catchy pop melodies. "Like a Prayer" received critical acclaim and solidified her reputation as an artist unafraid to confront and challenge societal norms.

Throughout the 1990s, Madonna continued to evolve as an artist and public figure. Her 1992 album "Erotica" and its accompanying book "Sex" pushed the boundaries of sexuality in popular culture. While the explicit content sparked controversy and backlash, it also opened up conversations about sexual expression and freedom. Madonna's willingness to explore and express her sexuality publicly was groundbreaking and influenced future generations of artists.

In 1998, Madonna released the critically acclaimed album "Ray of Light," which marked a departure from her previous work. The album incorporated electronic and dance music elements and featured introspective lyrics that reflected her interest in spirituality and self-discovery. Hits like "Frozen," "Ray of Light," and "The Power of Good-Bye" showcased a more mature and reflective side of Madonna. The album received widespread acclaim and won several Grammy Awards, further cementing her status as a music icon.

The early 2000s saw Madonna continue to innovate and adapt to changing musical trends. Her albums "Music" (2000) and "American Life" (2003) explored themes of fame, politics, and personal identity. "Music" featured the hit title track and the country-infused "Don't Tell Me," while "American Life" tackled issues such as the American dream and the impact of consumerism. Madonna's ability to address contemporary issues in her music demonstrated her relevance and adaptability in an ever-changing industry.

In addition to her music career, Madonna's influence extended to philanthropy and activism. She founded the charity Raising Malawi in 2006 to support orphans and vulnerable children in Malawi. Her efforts in humanitarian work, particularly in Africa, have made a significant impact and showcased her commitment to making a difference in the world. Madonna's philanthropic endeavors reflect her belief in using her platform for positive change and addressing global issues.

Madonna's later albums, such as "Confessions on a Dance Floor" (2005) and "Hard Candy" (2008), continued to demonstrate her ability to create danceable, catchy pop music. "Confessions on a Dance Floor," with its disco-inspired sound, produced hits like "Hung Up" and "Sorry," and received critical acclaim for its cohesive production and infectious energy. "Hard Candy" featured collaborations with contemporary artists such as Justin Timberlake and Timbaland, blending pop and hip-hop influences.

In recent years, Madonna has continued to push artistic boundaries and remain a relevant force in the music industry. Her 2012 album "MDNA" and its accompanying tour showcased her enduring appeal and ability to captivate audiences. The album featured hits like "Give Me All Your Luvin'" and "Girl Gone Wild," demonstrating her continued ability to create catchy, danceable music.

Madonna's influence on popular culture is undeniable. She has inspired countless artists across genres, including Britney Spears, Lady Gaga, Beyoncé, and Rihanna, who have cited her as a major influence on their own careers. Her ability to constantly reinvent herself and challenge societal norms has left a lasting impact on the music industry and beyond. Madonna's fearlessness in addressing issues such as sexuality, gender, and religion in her work has paved the way for greater acceptance and understanding of diverse perspectives in popular culture.

Madonna's legacy is not only defined by her music but also by her impact on fashion and style. Her bold and often provocative fashion choices have made her a fashion icon, influencing trends and setting new standards for self-expression. From her early days of lace gloves and crucifixes to her later collaborations with high-profile designers like Jean-Paul Gaultier and Dolce & Gabbana, Madonna's fashion evolution has been as dynamic and influential as her music.

In addition to her musical and fashion influence, Madonna has also made significant contributions to the film and television industry. Her production company, Maverick, has produced successful films and television shows, further showcasing her versatility and business acumen. Madonna's ability to navigate multiple facets of the entertainment industry with success is a testament to her multifaceted talent and relentless drive.

Chapter 44: Prince

Prince Rogers Nelson, known mononymously as Prince, was an American singer, songwriter, musician, record producer, dancer, actor, and filmmaker. Born on June 7, 1958, in Minneapolis, Minnesota, Prince emerged as one of the most talented, innovative, and influential artists in the history of popular music. Over the course of his prolific career, Prince released an extensive catalog of music that spanned multiple genres, including funk, rock, R&B, soul, new wave, and pop, and he became known for his flamboyant stage presence, wide vocal range, and virtuosic ability on multiple instruments. His work ethic, creativity, and unique artistic vision have left an indelible mark on the music industry and popular culture.

Prince was born into a musical family; his father, John L. Nelson, was a jazz pianist and songwriter, and his mother, Mattie Della Shaw, was a jazz singer. Named after his father's stage name, Prince Rogers, Prince showed an early aptitude for music. He taught himself to play piano at age seven and guitar at thirteen. His parents' influence and his exposure to a variety of musical styles in Minneapolis, a city with a rich and diverse musical scene, profoundly shaped his musical development.

Prince formed his first band, Grand Central (later renamed Champagne), during high school, where he played alongside his cousin and future members of his later bands. By the time he was a teenager, Prince had become a proficient multi-instrumentalist, playing keyboards, drums, bass, and guitar. His early recordings caught the attention of local producer Chris Moon, who helped him create a demo tape that eventually led to a recording contract with Warner Bros. Records in 1978, when Prince was just 19 years old.

Prince's debut album, "For You" (1978), showcased his prodigious talent and his insistence on creative control; he played all 27 instruments on the album and produced it himself. Though the album did not achieve significant commercial success, it set the stage for

Prince's career and demonstrated his potential. His second album, "Prince" (1979), fared better, producing the hit singles "Why You Wanna Treat Me So Bad?" and "I Wanna Be Your Lover," the latter of which reached number one on the Billboard Hot R&B Songs chart and crossed over to the pop charts. This album solidified Prince's reputation as a rising star in the music industry.

The early 1980s marked a period of rapid creative growth and commercial success for Prince. His third album, "Dirty Mind" (1980), was a departure from his earlier work, featuring a raw, minimalist sound and sexually explicit lyrics. The album received critical acclaim and established Prince as a bold and provocative artist. His next album, "Controversy" (1981), continued in a similar vein, blending rock, funk, and new wave influences and addressing themes of politics, religion, and sexuality.

Prince's breakthrough came with the release of his fifth album, "1999" (1982), which catapulted him to international stardom. The double album featured hits like "1999," "Little Red Corvette," and "Delirious," and showcased Prince's ability to create infectious, danceable tracks with socially conscious lyrics. The album's success was fueled by his groundbreaking use of synthesizers and drum machines, which helped define the sound of 1980s pop music.

In 1984, Prince reached the pinnacle of his career with the release of "Purple Rain," both the album and the film of the same name. "Purple Rain" was a critical and commercial triumph, selling over 25 million copies worldwide and earning Prince an Academy Award for Best Original Song Score. The album produced several hit singles, including "When Doves Cry," "Let's Go Crazy," and the iconic title track, "Purple Rain." The film, a semi-autobiographical story about a young musician's rise to fame, showcased Prince's talents as a performer and actor, and further solidified his status as a cultural icon.

Following the success of "Purple Rain," Prince continued to release a series of critically acclaimed and commercially successful albums throughout the 1980s, including "Around the World in a Day" (1985), "Parade" (1986), and "Sign o' the Times" (1987). These albums demonstrated Prince's versatility and willingness to experiment with different musical styles and genres. "Sign o' the Times," in particular, is often regarded as one of his masterpieces, blending funk, rock, soul, and social commentary into a cohesive and innovative double album.

Prince's prolific output extended beyond his own albums; he was also a prolific songwriter and producer for other artists. He wrote and produced hits for artists such as Sheila E., The Time, Vanity 6, and Apollonia 6, and he penned the iconic song "Nothing Compares 2 U," which became a massive hit for Sinéad O'Connor in 1990. His ability to craft hits for himself and others showcased his exceptional songwriting talent and his influence on the broader music industry.

In the early 1990s, Prince's relationship with his record label, Warner Bros., became increasingly strained. Frustrated by what he saw as limitations on his artistic freedom and disputes over the ownership of his master recordings, Prince famously changed his name to an unpronounceable symbol (often referred to as the "Love Symbol") in 1993. During this period, he was often referred to as "The Artist Formerly Known as Prince" or simply "The Artist." He also began releasing a series of albums at a rapid pace, aiming to fulfill his contract with Warner Bros. while exploring new musical directions.

Despite the challenges of his battles with the record label, Prince's creativity and output remained undiminished. He continued to release innovative and eclectic albums, including "The Gold Experience" (1995) and "Emancipation" (1996). "Emancipation," a triple album, marked his newfound freedom from his contract with Warner Bros. and showcased his diverse musical influences, from R&B and funk to rock and pop. The album was a commercial success and received critical acclaim for its ambitious scope and creativity.

The late 1990s and early 2000s saw Prince exploring new avenues for distributing his music. He was an early adopter of the internet as a means of connecting directly with his fans and releasing his work independently. His album "Crystal Ball" (1998) was initially sold exclusively through his website, demonstrating his willingness to embrace new technologies and business models. This approach allowed him greater control over his music and how it was presented to the world.

Prince's live performances during this period were legendary, characterized by their energy, spontaneity, and musicianship. He was known for his ability to play multiple instruments at a virtuoso level, and his concerts often featured extended jams and unexpected cover songs. His "Musicology" tour in 2004 was one of the highest-grossing tours of the year and introduced a new generation to his music. The accompanying album, "Musicology," received critical acclaim and marked a return to a more mainstream sound, blending elements of funk, R&B, and pop.

Throughout his career, Prince was also known for his philanthropic efforts and commitment to social justice. He quietly supported numerous charitable causes and organizations, often without seeking public recognition. He was a vocal advocate for artists' rights and fought for greater control over his music and legacy. His influence extended beyond music to issues of race, gender, and sexuality, and he used his platform to challenge societal norms and inspire positive change.

In the 2010s, Prince continued to release new music and perform live, remaining a vital and dynamic presence in the music world. His albums "20Ten" (2010), "Art Official Age" (2014), and "HITnRUN Phase One" and "HITnRUN Phase Two" (both released in 2015) showcased his enduring creativity and ability to evolve with the times. He continued to tour and perform, often playing marathon sets that demonstrated his incredible stamina and passion for music.

Prince's sudden death on April 21, 2016, at the age of 57, shocked and saddened fans around the world. He was found unresponsive at his Paisley Park estate in Chanhassen, Minnesota, and the cause of death was later determined to be an accidental overdose of fentanyl. His passing was a profound loss to the music community, but his legacy endures through his vast and diverse body of work.

Prince's influence on music, fashion, and culture is immeasurable. He broke down barriers and defied conventions, challenging traditional notions of race, gender, and sexuality. His eclectic style and willingness to experiment with different genres set new standards for artistic expression and creativity. Prince's ability to blend funk, rock, R&B, and pop into a unique and cohesive sound influenced countless artists across multiple genres, from Michael Jackson and Madonna to Beyoncé and Bruno Mars.

Prince's contributions to fashion and style were equally significant. His flamboyant stage outfits, featuring ruffled shirts, sequins, and bold colors, became iconic and influenced fashion trends for decades. His androgynous appearance and fluid approach to gender norms challenged societal expectations and inspired a more inclusive and open-minded view of identity and self-expression.

Prince's impact extended beyond his music and style; he was a visionary who changed the way artists approached their craft and their careers. His fight for artistic freedom and control over his work paved the way for future generations of musicians to assert their rights and pursue their creative visions without compromise. His innovative use of technology and independent distribution methods demonstrated the potential for artists to connect directly with their fans and retain control over their music.

Chapter 45: Tina Turner

Tina Turner, born Anna Mae Bullock on November 26, 1939, in Nutbush, Tennessee, is a legendary figure in the world of music and entertainment. Renowned as the "Queen of Rock 'n' Roll," Turner is celebrated for her powerful voice, electrifying stage presence, and a career that has spanned more than five decades. Her journey from a small-town girl in Tennessee to an international music icon is a remarkable story of talent, resilience, and reinvention.

Tina Turner's early life was marked by hardship and challenges. She was the youngest daughter of Floyd Richard Bullock, a sharecropper overseer, and Zelma Priscilla, a factory worker. Her parents had a tumultuous relationship, and after they separated, Tina and her sister were sent to live with their grandmother in Brownsville, Tennessee. Despite these early struggles, Tina found solace in music, singing in the church choir and developing a deep love for rhythm and blues.

In the late 1950s, Tina moved to St. Louis, Missouri, where her life would take a dramatic turn. She began frequenting local nightclubs, where she first encountered Ike Turner and his band, the Kings of Rhythm. Tina was captivated by Ike's musical talent and soon became a regular performer with the band. Her powerful voice and dynamic stage presence quickly made her a standout. It wasn't long before she and Ike became romantically involved and formed a professional partnership that would bring them both fame and success.

In 1960, Ike and Tina Turner recorded "A Fool in Love," which became a hit and launched their career as a duo. Their high-energy performances and Tina's electrifying presence on stage earned them a loyal following. Over the next decade, Ike and Tina Turner produced a string of hits, including "River Deep – Mountain High," "Proud Mary," and "Nutbush City Limits." Their success was not limited to the United States; they achieved international fame, performing to sold-out audiences around the world.

Despite their professional success, Tina Turner's personal life was marred by the abusive and tumultuous relationship with Ike. Ike's controlling behavior and physical abuse took a severe toll on Tina, but she endured for the sake of their career and their children. In 1976, after years of suffering, Tina finally found the courage to leave Ike, walking out with only 36 cents and a Mobil credit card. This decision marked the beginning of a new chapter in her life, both personally and professionally.

The late 1970s and early 1980s were a period of struggle for Tina Turner as she worked to rebuild her career. She performed in small clubs and made guest appearances on television shows, but it was not until the release of her 1984 album "Private Dancer" that she made a triumphant comeback. The album was a critical and commercial success, featuring hits like "What's Love Got to Do with It," "Better Be Good to Me," and the title track, "Private Dancer." "What's Love Got to Do with It" became Tina's signature song, earning her multiple Grammy Awards, including Record of the Year.

"Private Dancer" marked a turning point in Tina Turner's career, establishing her as a solo superstar and one of the most powerful voices in rock and pop music. Her subsequent albums, including "Break Every Rule" (1986) and "Foreign Affair" (1989), continued to build on her success, featuring hits like "Typical Male," "The Best," and "I Don't Wanna Lose You." Tina's ability to convey deep emotion and connect with her audience through her music set her apart from her contemporaries and solidified her status as a music legend.

In addition to her music career, Tina Turner also made a significant impact in film and television. She starred in the 1985 film "Mad Max Beyond Thunderdome," alongside Mel Gibson, and recorded the hit song "We Don't Need Another Hero" for the film's soundtrack. Her performance in the film showcased her versatility as an entertainer and further expanded her global appeal. In 1993, her life story was brought to the big screen in the biographical film "What's Love Got to Do with

It," starring Angela Bassett as Tina and Laurence Fishburne as Ike. The film was a critical and commercial success, earning Academy Award nominations for both Bassett and Fishburne and bringing Tina's story of resilience and triumph to a new generation of fans.

Throughout the 1990s and 2000s, Tina Turner continued to tour and perform, captivating audiences with her electrifying stage presence and powerful voice. Her "Wildest Dreams" (1996) and "Twenty Four Seven" (1999) tours were massive successes, solidifying her reputation as one of the greatest live performers in music history. In 2008, Tina embarked on her "Tina!: 50th Anniversary Tour," celebrating five decades in the music industry. The tour was a resounding success, earning rave reviews and breaking box office records.

Tina Turner's influence extends beyond her music and performances. She has been a trailblazer for women in the music industry, breaking barriers and setting new standards for female artists. Her ability to reinvent herself and maintain relevance across multiple decades is a testament to her talent, determination, and adaptability. Tina's distinctive voice, characterized by its raw power and emotional depth, has inspired countless artists, including Beyoncé, Whitney Houston, and Janet Jackson.

In addition to her musical achievements, Tina Turner has also made significant contributions to literature. She has authored several books, including her memoir "I, Tina" (1986), co-written with Kurt Loder, which provided an unflinching account of her life, her abusive marriage to Ike Turner, and her journey to reclaim her independence and career. The memoir was a bestseller and served as the basis for the 1993 film "What's Love Got to Do with It." In 2018, she published "My Love Story," a candid autobiography that delved deeper into her personal life, including her battle with health issues and her relationship with her longtime partner and husband, Erwin Bach.

Tina Turner's resilience and strength have also been evident in her personal life. After her divorce from Ike, she faced numerous challenges, including financial difficulties and health issues. However, she persevered, finding love and stability with Erwin Bach, a German music executive. The couple relocated to Switzerland, where they have lived for many years. Tina became a Swiss citizen in 2013, renouncing her American citizenship. Her personal journey of overcoming adversity and finding peace and happiness has been an inspiration to many.

Throughout her career, Tina Turner has received numerous accolades and honors. She has won a total of eight Grammy Awards and has been inducted into the Rock and Roll Hall of Fame twice, first as part of Ike & Tina Turner in 1991 and then as a solo artist in 2021. She has also received a Grammy Lifetime Achievement Award, a Kennedy Center Honor, and the Billboard Century Award, among many other honors. These accolades are a testament to her enduring impact on the music industry and her legacy as one of the greatest artists of all time.

In addition to her musical and literary contributions, Tina Turner has also been involved in various philanthropic efforts. She has supported numerous charitable organizations and causes, including children's health, HIV/AIDS research, and disaster relief efforts. Her commitment to giving back and making a positive impact on the world reflects her generous spirit and her belief in the power of compassion and community.

Tina Turner's influence on popular culture is immeasurable. Her music, characterized by its raw energy, emotional depth, and powerful vocals, has resonated with audiences around the world. Her iconic songs, such as "Proud Mary," "What's Love Got to Do with It," and "The Best," have become anthems of resilience, empowerment, and self-discovery. Tina's ability to convey deep emotion and connect with her audience through her music has made her a beloved figure and a true icon.

Chapter 46: David Lynch

David Lynch, born David Keith Lynch on January 20, 1946, in Missoula, Montana, is an American filmmaker, painter, musician, and writer who is widely regarded as one of the most innovative and influential directors in contemporary cinema. Known for his surrealist and often disturbing visual style, Lynch's work delves into the realms of dream logic, the subconscious, and the uncanny, creating films that are both enigmatic and captivating. His distinctive approach to storytelling and visual art has earned him a dedicated following and a reputation as a master of modern surrealism.

Lynch's early life was marked by frequent relocations due to his father's job as a research scientist for the U.S. Department of Agriculture. Despite these moves, Lynch's childhood was relatively stable, and he developed an early interest in drawing and painting. This passion for visual art led him to study at the School of the Museum of Fine Arts in Boston and later at the Pennsylvania Academy of the Fine Arts in Philadelphia. It was during his time in Philadelphia that Lynch began to experiment with moving images, creating short films that showcased his penchant for the bizarre and the surreal.

Lynch's first significant foray into filmmaking came with the production of his short film "The Alphabet" (1968), which combined live-action and animation to create a nightmarish vision of a child's alphabet lesson. The film's unsettling imagery and abstract narrative caught the attention of the American Film Institute (AFI), which invited Lynch to study at its Center for Advanced Film Studies in Los Angeles. It was here that Lynch began work on his first feature film, "Eraserhead" (1977).

"Eraserhead" is a deeply surreal and disturbing film that tells the story of Henry Spencer, a man living in a bleak, industrial landscape who must care for his deformed, alien-like child. The film's haunting visuals, eerie sound design, and disjointed narrative structure immediately set Lynch apart as a unique and visionary filmmaker. Despite its limited initial release, "Eraserhead" gradually gained a cult following and established Lynch as a rising talent in the world of independent cinema.

The success of "Eraserhead" caught the attention of producer Mel Brooks, who hired Lynch to direct the critically acclaimed film "The Elephant Man" (1980). Based on the true story of Joseph Merrick, a severely deformed man living in Victorian England, "The Elephant Man" was a departure from Lynch's earlier work in terms of its more conventional narrative structure. However, it still contained many of Lynch's signature elements, such as striking visuals, a focus on the grotesque, and a deep empathy for society's outsiders. The film was a commercial and critical success, earning eight Academy Award nominations, including Best Director for Lynch.

Following the success of "The Elephant Man," Lynch was given the opportunity to direct the big-budget science fiction film "Dune" (1984), based on Frank Herbert's classic novel. However, the production was plagued with difficulties, including studio interference and a rushed schedule. The resulting film was a critical and commercial failure, and Lynch later disowned the project, citing the lack of creative control as a significant factor in its shortcomings. Despite this setback, "Dune" has since gained a cult following, and some critics have reevaluated it more favorably over time.

Lynch rebounded from the disappointment of "Dune" with the release of "Blue Velvet" (1986), a film that has come to be regarded as one of his masterpieces. "Blue Velvet" tells the story of Jeffrey Beaumont, a college student who discovers a severed human ear in a field and becomes embroiled in a dark and twisted mystery involving a nightclub singer named Dorothy Vallens and a violent psychopath named Frank Booth. The film's blend of noir elements, surrealist imagery, and disturbing themes struck a chord with audiences and critics alike. "Blue Velvet" earned Lynch his second Academy Award nomination for Best Director and solidified his reputation as a daring and original filmmaker.

In the late 1980s and early 1990s, Lynch continued to push the boundaries of conventional filmmaking with a series of projects that further explored his fascination with the surreal and the macabre. One of his most notable achievements during this period was the creation of the television series "Twin Peaks" (1990-1991), which he co-created with writer Mark Frost. "Twin Peaks" is set in a small, seemingly idyllic town in the Pacific Northwest, where the murder of high school student Laura Palmer sets off a chain of events that uncover the town's many dark secrets. The show's unique blend of mystery, melodrama, and supernatural elements captivated audiences and became a cultural phenomenon. "Twin Peaks" was praised for its innovative storytelling, quirky characters, and haunting atmosphere, and it has since been regarded as one of the greatest television series of all time.

In addition to "Twin Peaks," Lynch continued to create feature films that challenged and intrigued audiences. "Wild at Heart" (1990), based on the novel by Barry Gifford, is a violent and darkly comic road movie that won the Palme d'Or at the Cannes Film Festival. "Twin Peaks: Fire Walk with Me" (1992), a prequel to the television series, delves deeper into the life and death of Laura Palmer, offering a more explicit and disturbing portrayal of the events leading up to her murder. Although "Fire Walk with Me" was initially met with mixed reviews, it has since gained a more appreciative audience and is considered an essential part of the "Twin Peaks" saga.

The late 1990s and early 2000s saw Lynch continuing to explore the themes and stylistic elements that had become his trademarks. "Lost Highway" (1997) is a neo-noir thriller that blurs the lines between reality and fantasy, following the story of a jazz musician who is accused of murder and then inexplicably transforms into a different person. "The Straight Story" (1999) is a departure from Lynch's usual style, telling the true story of Alvin Straight, an elderly man who travels across the Midwest on a lawnmower to visit his estranged brother. The film is notable for its straightforward narrative and heartfelt tone, earning Lynch widespread acclaim and proving his versatility as a filmmaker.

"Mulholland Drive" (2001) is another of Lynch's most celebrated works, a dreamlike and enigmatic film that explores the dark underbelly of Hollywood. The film follows the story of an aspiring actress named Betty Elms and an amnesiac woman who together try to unravel the mystery of the latter's identity. "Mulholland Drive" is noted for its nonlinear narrative, surreal imagery, and ambiguous ending, which have inspired countless interpretations and analyses. The film earned Lynch his third Academy Award nomination for Best Director and has been hailed as one of the greatest films of the 21st century.

In 2006, Lynch released "Inland Empire," an experimental film that further pushed the boundaries of conventional storytelling and visual style. Shot on digital video and featuring a fragmented, nonlinear narrative, "Inland Empire" tells the story of an actress named Nikki Grace, whose life begins to blur with the character she is playing in a film. The film's three-hour runtime, abstract structure, and disorienting visuals make it one of Lynch's most challenging works, but it has also been praised for its audacity and artistic vision.

Beyond his work in film and television, Lynch is also a prolific visual artist and musician. His paintings, drawings, and photographs often explore similar themes to his films, featuring dark, surreal imagery and a fascination with the subconscious. Lynch has held numerous exhibitions of his visual art, and his work has been featured in galleries and museums around the world. As a musician, Lynch has released several albums, including "Crazy Clown Time" (2011) and "The Big Dream" (2013), which showcase his eclectic taste and experimental approach to sound.

Lynch's contributions to the world of cinema and art have been widely recognized and celebrated. He has received numerous awards and honors, including an honorary Academy Award in 2019 for his contributions to the art of film. Lynch's influence can be seen in the work of countless filmmakers, artists, and musicians who have been inspired by his unique vision and fearless creativity.

In addition to his artistic endeavors, Lynch is also a dedicated advocate for Transcendental Meditation (TM), a practice he has followed since the 1970s. He founded the David Lynch Foundation in 2005, which aims to promote TM as a means of improving mental health and well-being, particularly for at-risk populations such as veterans, victims of domestic violence, and students in underserved communities. Lynch's commitment to TM and his efforts to share its benefits with others reflect his belief in the power of meditation to bring peace and creativity into people's lives.

David Lynch's impact on the world of film and art is profound and far-reaching. His ability to create immersive, otherworldly experiences that challenge conventional storytelling and explore the depths of the human psyche has set him apart as one of the most distinctive and influential voices in contemporary cinema. Lynch's work invites viewers to embrace the unknown, question reality, and delve into the mysteries of the subconscious. His legacy as a filmmaker, artist, and visionary continues to inspire and captivate audiences around the world, and his contributions to the arts will undoubtedly be remembered for generations to come.

Chapter 47: Quentin Tarantino

Quentin Tarantino, born on March 27, 1963, in Knoxville, Tennessee, is an American filmmaker, screenwriter, and actor known for his unique storytelling style, non-linear narratives, and extensive use of pop culture references. His influence on modern cinema is profound, marked by a distinctive blend of violence, dark humor, and sharp dialogue. Tarantino's early life was steeped in movies and television, fostering a deep passion for storytelling. His mother, Connie McHugh, and stepfather, Curtis Zastoupil, supported his early interest in film, often taking him to see a wide variety of movies, ranging from mainstream hits to obscure cult classics. This eclectic exposure to different genres would later become a hallmark of his work.

Tarantino dropped out of high school at the age of 15, opting instead to attend acting classes and work at a video rental store, Video Archives, in Manhattan Beach, California. It was here that he met several like-minded individuals and began to develop his screenwriting skills. His encyclopedic knowledge of films and his passion for storytelling made him a favorite among customers and colleagues alike. This period of his life was crucial in shaping his cinematic style, as he immersed himself in a vast array of films, dissecting them and learning from their successes and failures.

Tarantino's breakthrough came with the release of "Reservoir Dogs" in 1992, a heist film that captivated audiences and critics alike with its sharp dialogue, unconventional structure, and brutal violence. The film was a sensation at the Sundance Film Festival and marked the arrival of a new, audacious voice in American cinema. "Reservoir Dogs" showcased Tarantino's ability to blend genres and create memorable characters, traits that would become defining features of his work.

His next film, "Pulp Fiction," released in 1994, cemented his status as one of the most innovative and influential directors of his generation. "Pulp Fiction" is widely regarded as a masterpiece, with its intertwining narratives, unforgettable characters, and iconic dialogue. The film won the Palme d'Or at the Cannes Film Festival and earned Tarantino an Academy Award for Best Original Screenplay. "Pulp Fiction" also played a significant role in reviving the career of John Travolta, who delivered a standout performance as Vincent Vega.

Following the success of "Pulp Fiction," Tarantino continued to push the boundaries of conventional filmmaking with "Jackie Brown" (1997), an adaptation of Elmore Leonard's novel "Rum Punch." The film, starring Pam Grier and Samuel L. Jackson, was a homage to the blaxploitation films of the 1970s and showcased Tarantino's ability to craft compelling stories with complex characters. Although "Jackie Brown" was not as commercially successful as its predecessor, it was critically acclaimed and further demonstrated Tarantino's versatility as a filmmaker.

In the early 2000s, Tarantino embarked on a new creative venture with the "Kill Bill" series, a two-part epic that paid homage to martial arts films, spaghetti westerns, and exploitation cinema. "Kill Bill: Vol. 1" (2003) and "Kill Bill: Vol. 2" (2004) starred Uma Thurman as The Bride, a former assassin seeking revenge against her former colleagues. The films were noted for their stylized violence, intricate fight choreography, and a rich tapestry of references to various film genres. The "Kill Bill" series further solidified Tarantino's reputation as a master of genre blending and visual storytelling.

Tarantino's next major project was "Inglourious Basterds" (2009), a revisionist history war film set during World War II. The film follows a group of Jewish-American soldiers known as the "Basterds" who embark on a mission to kill as many Nazis as possible. "Inglourious Basterds" was praised for its bold narrative choices, particularly its reimagining of historical events, and featured standout performances from Brad Pitt and Christoph Waltz. Waltz, in particular, received widespread acclaim for his portrayal of Colonel Hans Landa, earning an Academy Award for Best Supporting Actor. The film was a commercial and critical success, further cementing Tarantino's status as a visionary filmmaker.

In 2012, Tarantino released "Django Unchained," a western set in the Antebellum South that tackled the brutal realities of slavery through the lens of genre cinema. The film starred Jamie Foxx as Django, a freed slave on a quest to rescue his wife from a ruthless plantation owner, played by Leonardo DiCaprio. "Django Unchained" was both a critical and commercial success, earning Tarantino his second Academy Award for Best Original Screenplay. The film's bold approach to sensitive historical subject matter sparked debate, but it also highlighted Tarantino's ability to address serious themes within the framework of entertaining and provocative cinema.

Tarantino continued to explore the western genre with "The Hateful Eight" (2015), a chamber piece set in post-Civil War Wyoming. The film brought together an ensemble cast, including Samuel L. Jackson, Kurt Russell, and Jennifer Jason Leigh, in a tense, dialogue-driven narrative. "The Hateful Eight" was noted for its stunning cinematography, shot in Ultra Panavision 70mm, and its intricate plot structure. While it received mixed reviews from some critics, it was praised for its performances and Tarantino's skillful direction.

In 2019, Tarantino released "Once Upon a Time in Hollywood," a nostalgic homage to the Golden Age of Hollywood set in 1969. The film starred Leonardo DiCaprio as a fading television actor and Brad Pitt as his stunt double, navigating the changing landscape of the film industry. "Once Upon a Time in Hollywood" was lauded for its meticulous recreation of the era, its blend of historical and fictional elements, and the performances of its lead actors. The film earned numerous accolades, including an Academy Award for Brad Pitt and a Golden Globe for Tarantino's screenplay.

Throughout his career, Quentin Tarantino has been a polarizing figure, often sparking debates about his use of violence and controversial subject matter. However, his impact on modern cinema is undeniable. His films are characterized by their sharp wit, memorable characters, and a deep love for the art of filmmaking. Tarantino's ability to blend genres, create intricate narratives, and pay homage to his cinematic influences while crafting something entirely unique has set him apart as a true auteur.

Tarantino has often spoken about his intention to retire after completing ten films, wanting to leave the audience wanting more rather than overstaying his welcome. As of now, with nine films under his belt, the film world eagerly anticipates what his final project will be. Regardless of what the future holds, Quentin Tarantino's legacy is secure, and his films will continue to be studied, celebrated, and debated for generations to come. His work has not only entertained millions but also inspired countless filmmakers to pursue their own creative visions, making him one of the most significant figures in contemporary cinema.

Chapter 48: Tim Burton

Tim Burton, born Timothy Walter Burton on August 25, 1958, in Burbank, California, is an American filmmaker, artist, writer, and animator renowned for his distinctive visual style and penchant for blending macabre and whimsical elements. Growing up in the heart of the entertainment industry, Burton was drawn to art and cinema from an early age. His childhood was marked by a fascination with classic horror films, comic books, and the works of Edgar Allan Poe, all of which would profoundly influence his creative sensibilities.

Burton's early years were spent as something of an outsider, preferring to immerse himself in his vivid imagination rather than engaging with the world around him. This sense of being an outsider became a recurring theme in his work, often manifesting in protagonists who are misunderstood or out of place in their surroundings. After high school, he attended the California Institute of the Arts (CalArts), where he studied animation. His unique artistic vision quickly caught the attention of his professors and peers.

Upon graduation, Burton was hired by Walt Disney Studios as an apprentice animator. His tenure at Disney, however, was marked by frustration as his dark and quirky style clashed with the studio's more traditional approach. Despite this, he contributed to projects like "The Fox and the Hound" (1981) and "The Black Cauldron" (1985). During his time at Disney, Burton created the short film "Vincent" (1982), a stop-motion animated tribute to his idol Vincent Price. The short, narrated by Price himself, showcased Burton's talent for combining gothic elements with heartfelt storytelling. This was followed by another short film, "Frankenweenie" (1984), a live-action tale about a boy who reanimates his dead dog. Although "Frankenweenie" was initially deemed too dark for children and led to Burton's dismissal from Disney, it would later be recognized as a precursor to his future work.

Burton's breakthrough came with his first feature film, "Pee-wee's Big Adventure" (1985), a comedy about the eccentric man-child Pee-wee Herman, played by Paul Reubens. The film was a commercial success and established Burton's ability to balance humor and offbeat charm. Its success led to Burton directing "Beetlejuice" (1988), a darkly comedic fantasy about a recently deceased couple who hire a mischievous ghost to scare away the new inhabitants of their home. "Beetlejuice" was both a critical and commercial success, further cementing Burton's reputation as a director with a unique and imaginative style.

In 1989, Burton directed "Batman," a dark and brooding take on the iconic comic book character. Starring Michael Keaton as Batman and Jack Nicholson as the Joker, the film was a massive box office hit and a cultural phenomenon. Burton's vision for Gotham City, with its gothic architecture and shadowy streets, became a defining feature of the Batman mythos. The success of "Batman" led to a sequel, "Batman Returns" (1992), which delved even deeper into Burton's dark and stylized aesthetic. The film featured memorable performances by Danny DeVito as the Penguin and Michelle Pfeiffer as Catwoman, and although it was darker and more divisive than its predecessor, it further showcased Burton's distinctive directorial voice.

In between the two Batman films, Burton directed "Edward Scissorhands" (1990), a modern fairy tale about a gentle, artificial man with scissors for hands, played by Johnny Depp. The film, which also starred Winona Ryder and Dianne Wiest, was a critical and commercial success. "Edward Scissorhands" marked the beginning of a long and fruitful collaboration between Burton and Depp, with Depp becoming Burton's frequent leading man. The film's poignant exploration of isolation and acceptance, combined with its striking visual design, made it one of Burton's most beloved works.

The early 1990s saw Burton return to his animation roots with "The Nightmare Before Christmas" (1993), a stop-motion animated musical that he produced and conceived, with Henry Selick directing. The film follows Jack Skellington, the Pumpkin King of Halloween Town, who discovers Christmas Town and becomes obsessed with celebrating the holiday. "The Nightmare Before Christmas" has since become a cult classic, celebrated for its innovative animation, memorable characters, and hauntingly beautiful music by Danny Elfman, another frequent Burton collaborator.

Burton continued to explore his unique blend of the macabre and whimsical with "Ed Wood" (1994), a biographical film about the notoriously inept filmmaker of the same name. Starring Johnny Depp as Ed Wood and Martin Landau as Bela Lugosi, the film was a labor of love for Burton, who identified with Wood's outsider status and unyielding passion for filmmaking. Although "Ed Wood" was not a box office success, it received critical acclaim and earned Landau an Academy Award for Best Supporting Actor.

The late 1990s and early 2000s saw Burton tackle a variety of projects, each marked by his signature style. "Mars Attacks!" (1996), a satirical science fiction film based on a series of trading cards, featured an ensemble cast and showcased Burton's penchant for blending dark humor with absurdity. "Sleepy Hollow" (1999), a gothic horror film based on Washington Irving's "The Legend of Sleepy Hollow," starred Johnny Depp as Ichabod Crane and was praised for its atmospheric visuals and chilling storytelling.

In 2001, Burton directed a reimagining of "Planet of the Apes," which, despite being a commercial success, received mixed reviews from critics and audiences. This was followed by "Big Fish" (2003), a fantasy drama that marked a departure from Burton's darker themes. The film, starring Ewan McGregor and Albert Finney, tells the story of a man trying to reconcile with his dying father through his fantastical tales. "Big Fish" was well-received and is often regarded as one of Burton's most emotionally resonant films.

Burton returned to animation with "Corpse Bride" (2005), a stop-motion animated film that he co-directed with Mike Johnson. The film, featuring the voices of Johnny Depp and Helena Bonham Carter, was praised for its stunning animation and darkly romantic story. In 2007, Burton directed an adaptation of the musical "Sweeney Todd: The Demon Barber of Fleet Street," starring Depp as the vengeful barber and Bonham Carter as his accomplice. The film was both a critical and commercial success, earning several Academy Award nominations and solidifying Burton's reputation for bringing macabre stories to the screen with style and flair.

Burton's next major project was "Alice in Wonderland" (2010), a live-action/CGI hybrid adaptation of Lewis Carroll's classic tales. Starring Mia Wasikowska as Alice, Johnny Depp as the Mad Hatter, and Helena Bonham Carter as the Red Queen, the film was a visual spectacle that became a major box office hit. Although it received mixed reviews, its success led to a sequel, "Alice Through the Looking Glass" (2016), which Burton produced but did not direct.

In 2012, Burton directed "Dark Shadows," a gothic comedy based on the cult television series of the same name. Starring Johnny Depp as the vampire Barnabas Collins, the film featured an ensemble cast and Burton's trademark dark humor. Although "Dark Shadows" received mixed reviews, it further demonstrated Burton's ability to blend different genres and tones.

Burton returned to his roots with "Frankenweenie" (2012), a feature-length stop-motion animated remake of his earlier short film. The film, which tells the story of a boy who brings his beloved dog back to life, was praised for its heartwarming story and meticulous animation. "Frankenweenie" was nominated for an Academy Award for Best Animated Feature, showcasing Burton's enduring talent for creating emotionally resonant stories through animation.

In 2014, Burton directed "Big Eyes," a biographical drama about artist Margaret Keane, whose distinctive paintings of children with large eyes were fraudulently claimed by her husband, Walter Keane. Starring Amy Adams and Christoph Waltz, the film was a departure from Burton's typical style, focusing more on character and narrative than visual spectacle. "Big Eyes" was well-received, with particular praise for Adams' performance.

Burton's 2016 film, "Miss Peregrine's Home for Peculiar Children," based on the novel by Ransom Riggs, blended fantasy and adventure in a story about a boy who discovers a hidden orphanage for children with supernatural abilities. The film was noted for its imaginative visuals and quirky characters, elements that are quintessentially Burton.

Throughout his career, Tim Burton has established himself as a singular voice in cinema, known for his ability to meld the whimsical with the macabre, the fantastical with the deeply human. His films often explore themes of isolation, acceptance, and the struggle to remain true to oneself in a conformist world. His collaborations with actors like Johnny Depp and Helena Bonham Carter, as well as composer Danny Elfman, have resulted in some of the most memorable and distinctive films of the past few decades.

Burton's influence extends beyond film; his distinctive visual style and storytelling approach have made him a cultural icon, inspiring artists and filmmakers across various mediums. His work continues to captivate audiences with its blend of dark humor, emotional depth, and boundless creativity, ensuring that Tim Burton's legacy will endure for generations to come.

Chapter 49: Hans Zimmer

Hans Zimmer, born on September 12, 1957, in Frankfurt am Main, West Germany, is a highly influential and prolific film composer known for his innovative use of electronic music and orchestral arrangements. Over a career spanning several decades, Zimmer has composed music for more than 150 films, earning numerous awards and accolades, including an Academy Award, two Golden Globes, and four Grammys. His work has had a profound impact on the film industry, helping to redefine the role of music in cinema and shaping the sound of modern film scores.

Zimmer's early years were marked by a passion for music and experimentation with various sounds. He began playing the piano at a young age, although he disliked formal lessons and preferred to learn by improvisation. His father, an engineer, died when Zimmer was still a child, and his mother, a musician, supported his musical pursuits. Zimmer's early influences included classical composers such as Johann Sebastian Bach and Ludwig van Beethoven, as well as contemporary electronic music pioneers like Kraftwerk and Tangerine Dream. This eclectic mix of influences would later become a hallmark of his work.

In the late 1970s, Zimmer moved to London, where he became involved in the music scene, working with various bands and artists. He played keyboards and synthesizers for the Buggles, a new wave band best known for their hit single "Video Killed the Radio Star," which became the first music video ever aired on MTV in 1981. Zimmer's work with the Buggles and other bands allowed him to hone his skills with electronic music and studio production, setting the stage for his future career in film scoring.

Zimmer's entry into the world of film music began in the early 1980s when he started working as an assistant to film composer Stanley Myers. Myers, best known for his work on "The Deer Hunter" (1978), took Zimmer under his wing and introduced him to the art of film scoring. Together, they composed scores for several films, blending traditional orchestration with electronic elements. One of their notable collaborations was the score for the film "My Beautiful Laundrette" (1985), which showcased Zimmer's emerging talent and innovative approach to music.

Zimmer's breakthrough as a solo composer came with the 1988 film "Rain Man," directed by Barry Levinson and starring Tom Cruise and Dustin Hoffman. The film, which tells the story of a man who discovers his estranged brother is an autistic savant, required a sensitive and unique musical approach. Zimmer's score, characterized by its minimalist piano themes and electronic textures, perfectly complemented the film's emotional and narrative depth. The success of "Rain Man" earned Zimmer his first Academy Award nomination and established him as a major force in the world of film music.

Following the success of "Rain Man," Zimmer's career took off, and he quickly became one of the most sought-after composers in Hollywood. In the 1990s, he scored a series of high-profile films, each showcasing his ability to blend different musical styles and create memorable, emotionally resonant scores. One of his most iconic works from this period is the score for "The Lion King" (1994), an animated Disney film that became a cultural phenomenon. Zimmer's score, which incorporated African musical elements and featured songs by Elton John and Tim Rice, won the Academy Award for Best Original Score and remains one of the most beloved film scores of all time.

Throughout the 1990s and early 2000s, Zimmer continued to push the boundaries of film music with his work on films such as "Crimson Tide" (1995), "The Rock" (1996), "Gladiator" (2000), and "Black Hawk Down" (2001). His score for "Gladiator," directed by Ridley Scott and starring Russell Crowe, was particularly noteworthy for its epic scope and emotional intensity. The score, which blended traditional orchestral elements with modern electronic sounds, earned

Zimmer another Academy Award nomination and helped to redefine the sound of the historical epic genre.

Zimmer's collaboration with director Christopher Nolan has been one of the most significant and fruitful partnerships of his career. Their first collaboration was on the film "Batman Begins" (2005), a reboot of the Batman franchise that marked a darker, more realistic take on the character. Zimmer, along with co-composer James Newton Howard, created a score that was both atmospheric and powerful, capturing the essence of Nolan's vision. This collaboration continued with "The Dark Knight" (2008) and "The Dark Knight Rises" (2012), with Zimmer's music playing a crucial role in the films' critical and commercial success. The score for "The Dark Knight," in particular, was praised for its innovative use of themes and motifs, including the iconic, tension-building two-note motif for the Joker, played by Heath Ledger.

Zimmer's work with Nolan extended beyond the Batman trilogy to include other groundbreaking films such as "Inception" (2010), "Interstellar" (2014), and "Dunkirk" (2017). The score for "Inception," with its use of the "Shepard tone" to create a sense of endless rising tension and its powerful, brass-heavy themes, became instantly iconic. "Interstellar" showcased Zimmer's ability to create a deeply emotional and otherworldly score, using a pipe organ and orchestral elements to evoke the vastness and mystery of space. For "Dunkirk," Zimmer crafted a relentlessly intense and immersive score, using minimalist motifs and innovative sound design to heighten the film's sense of urgency and suspense.

Zimmer's versatility as a composer is evident in his work across a wide range of genres and styles. He has scored everything from action-packed blockbusters like "Pirates of the Caribbean: The Curse of the Black Pearl" (2003) and its sequels, to intimate dramas like "Thelma & Louise" (1991) and "As Good as It Gets" (1997). His ability to adapt his musical style to fit the specific needs of each film has made him one of the most in-demand composers in the industry.

In addition to his work in film, Zimmer has also composed music for television, video games, and live performances. He scored the acclaimed BBC nature documentary series "Planet Earth II" (2016) and "Blue Planet II" (2017), creating lush, evocative soundscapes that complemented the stunning visuals. His work in video games includes the scores for "Call of Duty: Modern Warfare 2" (2009) and "Crysis 2" (2011), where he brought his cinematic sensibilities to the interactive medium. Zimmer has also toured extensively, performing his film music in concerts around the world, allowing audiences to experience his work in a live setting.

Zimmer's contributions to film music extend beyond his own compositions. He is the head of Remote Control Productions, a company that has nurtured and mentored a new generation of film composers, including Harry Gregson-Williams, John Powell, and Ramin Djawadi. Through Remote Control Productions, Zimmer has fostered a collaborative and innovative environment, pushing the boundaries of what film music can achieve.

Despite his many achievements, Zimmer remains a humble and dedicated artist, constantly seeking new challenges and opportunities to grow as a composer. He has spoken about the importance of collaboration in his work, emphasizing the role of the director, musicians, and other creatives in bringing a film score to life. Zimmer's willingness to experiment and take risks has kept his music fresh and relevant, ensuring that his work continues to resonate with audiences around the world.

In recent years, Zimmer has continued to deliver outstanding scores for films such as "Blade Runner 2049" (2017), co-composed with Benjamin Wallfisch, "Widows" (2018), "Dune" (2021), and "No Time to Die" (2021), the latest James Bond film. His score for "Blade Runner 2049," a sequel to Ridley Scott's 1982 classic, paid homage to the original's iconic music while introducing new, atmospheric elements that captured the film's futuristic vision. "Dune," directed by

Denis Villeneuve, showcased Zimmer's ability to create an epic and otherworldly soundscape, using a combination of traditional instruments, electronic sounds, and unique vocalizations to evoke the vastness and mystique of the film's desert planet.

Zimmer's influence on modern film music is immeasurable. His innovative use of electronic music, his ability to blend different genres and styles, and his knack for creating memorable, emotionally resonant themes have set new standards for what a film score can achieve. His work has inspired countless composers and musicians, and his impact on the industry will be felt for generations to come.

Hans Zimmer's career is a testament to the power of music in cinema. His scores have not only enhanced the films they accompany but have also become an integral part of the cultural zeitgeist. From the haunting melodies of "The Lion King" to the pulse-pounding rhythms of "Inception," Zimmer's music has left an indelible mark on the world of film, elevating the art of film scoring to new heights. As he continues to push the boundaries of his craft, there is no doubt that Hans Zimmer will remain a towering figure in the world of film music, inspiring future generations with his boundless creativity and passion for storytelling.

Chapter 50: Gustav Klimt

Gustav Klimt, born on July 14, 1862, in Baumgarten, near Vienna, Austria, is widely regarded as one of the most prominent and influential artists of the late 19th and early 20th centuries. As a key figure in the Vienna Secession movement, Klimt's work represents a bridge between traditional academic art and the emerging modernist styles of the 20th century. His distinctive style, characterized by bold patterns, sensuous figures, and the extensive use of gold leaf, has made him a celebrated and often controversial figure in the history of art.

Klimt was born into a lower-middle-class family; his father, Ernst Klimt, was a gold engraver, and his mother, Anna Klimt, had a passion for music. Gustav was the second of seven children, and from an early age, he displayed a talent for drawing. Recognizing his potential, his family encouraged him to pursue an artistic career. In 1876, at the age of 14, Klimt enrolled in the Vienna School of Arts and Crafts (Kunstgewerbeschule), where he studied until 1883. During his time at the school, he received a traditional academic training, which included rigorous instruction in drawing, painting, and the decorative arts.

After completing his studies, Klimt, along with his brother Ernst and their friend Franz Matsch, formed a company called the "Künstler-Compagnie" (Artists' Company). They received commissions to create murals and decorative works for a variety of public and private buildings, including theaters and museums. Some of their notable early projects included the murals for the Kunsthistorisches Museum and the ceiling paintings for the Burgtheater in Vienna. These early works adhered to the traditional academic style, showcasing Klimt's technical skill and his ability to work on a grand scale.

In the late 1880s and early 1890s, Klimt began to experiment with a more personal and expressive style. This period marked a turning point in his career as he started to move away from the conventional techniques he had mastered. The death of his father and brother in 1892 had a profound impact on him, leading to a period of introspection and artistic exploration. Klimt's work from this period began to reflect his interest in symbolism, mythology, and the female form, themes that would dominate his later work.

In 1897, Klimt became one of the founding members of the Vienna Secession, a group of artists who sought to break away from the conservative art establishment and promote a more modern and innovative approach to art. The Secessionists were influenced by a variety of artistic movements, including Symbolism, Art Nouveau, and the Arts and Crafts Movement. They aimed to create a total work of art (Gesamtkunstwerk) that integrated painting, sculpture, architecture, and the decorative arts. Klimt served as the first president of the Vienna Secession, and his leadership and vision helped to shape the direction of the movement.

One of Klimt's most significant contributions to the Vienna Secession was his role in organizing the group's exhibitions. These exhibitions were groundbreaking in their presentation and curation, often featuring a mix of traditional and avant-garde works. The Secessionists' first exhibition, held in 1898, included Klimt's "Pallas Athene," a striking painting that showcased his emerging style. The figure of Pallas Athene, the Greek goddess of wisdom and war, is depicted in a bold, almost abstract manner, with a golden helmet and an intense, enigmatic expression. This work marked the beginning of Klimt's fascination with gold and other metallic elements, which would become a hallmark of his mature style.

Klimt's "Golden Phase," which lasted from the late 1890s to the early 1900s, is perhaps his most famous and influential period. During this time, he created some of his most iconic works, characterized by the lavish use of gold leaf and intricate patterns. One of the earliest and most notable examples from this period is the "Portrait of Adele Bloch-Bauer I" (1907). Commissioned by Ferdinand Bloch-Bauer, a wealthy industrialist, the painting depicts his wife, Adele, adorned in an opulent gown decorated with gold and silver leaf. The portrait is a masterful fusion of realism and abstraction, with Adele's face and hands rendered with exquisite detail, while her dress and the background dissolve into a shimmering mosaic of geometric shapes and ornamental patterns.

Another seminal work from Klimt's Golden Phase is "The Kiss" (1907-1908), which has become one of the most recognizable and celebrated images in the history of art. The painting depicts a couple locked in an intimate embrace; their bodies enveloped in a cloak of golden patterns. The use of gold leaf, combined with the intricate, almost Byzantine-like detailing, creates a sense of timelessness and transcendence. "The Kiss" exemplifies Klimt's ability to convey deep emotion and sensuality through his unique visual language.

Klimt's fascination with the female form is evident throughout his oeuvre. He often portrayed women in a sensuous and intimate manner, exploring themes of love, beauty, and eroticism. His depictions of women were groundbreaking in their frankness and complexity, challenging the conventional representations of femininity in art. Works such as "Danaë" (1907) and "Judith and the Head of Holofernes" (1901) showcase his ability to blend mythological and biblical themes with a modern, psychological depth.

In addition to his paintings, Klimt was also an accomplished draftsman and produced a large number of drawings and sketches. These works on paper often reveal a more spontaneous and experimental side of his artistry. His drawings, particularly those of the female nude, are notable for their sensitivity and fluidity, capturing the essence of the human form with a few deft strokes. Klimt's drawings were often preparatory studies for his larger works, but they also stand alone as significant contributions to his body of work.

Klimt's impact on the art world extended beyond his own creations. As a leading figure of the Vienna Secession, he played a crucial role in fostering a vibrant and innovative artistic community in Vienna. The Secessionists' journal, "Ver Sacrum" (Sacred Spring), served as a platform for the exchange of ideas and the promotion of new artistic trends. Klimt's influence can be seen in the work of other artists associated with the Secession, including Egon Schiele and Oskar Kokoschka, who both admired and were inspired by his bold and expressive style.

Despite his success and recognition, Klimt's work was not without controversy. His candid depictions of sexuality and the female body often provoked criticism and scandal. In 1900, his ceiling paintings for the Great Hall of the University of Vienna, which included the works "Philosophy," "Medicine," and "Jurisprudence," were met with harsh criticism for their erotic content and perceived lack of clarity. The backlash from these commissions marked a turning point in Klimt's career, leading him to focus more on private commissions and his own artistic vision, free from the constraints of public approval.

Klimt's later years were marked by a continued exploration of new themes and techniques. He experimented with landscapes, creating a series of richly colored and textured paintings that showcased his love for nature. Works such as "The Park" (1909-1910) and "Farm Garden with Sunflowers" (1905-1906) reveal his mastery of color and composition, as well as his ability to capture the beauty and tranquility of the natural world.

Throughout his career, Klimt remained dedicated to the pursuit of artistic innovation and personal expression. His work defies easy categorization, blending elements of Symbolism, Art Nouveau, and early modernism into a unique and highly personal style. His influence can be seen in the work of countless artists who followed, and his legacy continues to resonate in the contemporary art world.

Gustav Klimt's life was relatively private, and he remained unmarried throughout his life, though he was known to have had several romantic relationships and fathered at least 14 children. He lived a modest life, devoted primarily to his art and his close-knit circle of family and friends. Despite his reclusive nature, Klimt was a central figure in the cultural life of Vienna, contributing significantly to the city's reputation as a hub of artistic and intellectual activity at the turn of the century.

Klimt's health began to decline in the early 1910s, and on February 6, 1918, he suffered a stroke that left him partially paralyzed. He died a few weeks later on February 6, 1918, at the age of 55. His death marked the end of an era, but his influence and legacy have endured. Today, Klimt's works are celebrated and cherished around the world, housed in major museums and private collections, and his name is synonymous with the innovation and beauty of early 20th-century art.

Epilogue

As we close the pages of *Profiles of Supremely Creative People*, we are left with a tapestry of human ingenuity and the enduring power of the creative spirit. The individuals we have journeyed with each represent a unique facet of creativity, a testament to the boundless ways in which imagination can shape our world.

These profiles are more than just biographies; they are chronicles of human potential. They remind us that creativity is not confined to a single domain or discipline but is a universal thread that weaves through all aspects of life. From the scientific breakthroughs of Marie Curie to the artistic revolutions of Pablo Picasso, we see that creativity knows no boundaries. It is an ever-present force, waiting to be harnessed, nurtured, and expressed.

What unites these diverse figures is not only their extraordinary achievements but also their shared traits: an insatiable curiosity, a relentless pursuit of their passions, and an unwavering belief in their visions. They faced obstacles, failures, and doubts, yet they persisted. Their stories are a powerful reminder that creativity often flourishes in the face of adversity.

As we reflect on their journeys, we are inspired to look within ourselves and recognize our own creative potential. Creativity is not reserved for the chosen few; it is a birthright of humanity. Each of us carries the spark of creativity, capable of igniting change, innovation, and beauty in the world.

In a rapidly evolving world, the need for creative thinking and innovation has never been greater. The challenges we face today require solutions that transcend conventional wisdom and embrace new perspectives. The stories in this book serve as a beacon, guiding us toward a future where creativity is not just an aspiration but a way of life.

Let us carry forward the legacy of these supremely creative individuals. Let their journeys inspire us to explore, to question, and to create. Whether we are artists, scientists, writers, entrepreneurs, or dreamers, let us embrace the spirit of creativity in all that we do.

The flame of creativity burns eternal, and it is up to us to keep it alight. As we step into the world, may we do so with the courage to dream, the passion to innovate, and the resilience to transform those dreams into reality.

Thank you for embarking on this journey with us. The stories of these remarkable individuals are now a part of our collective narrative, a testament to the extraordinary potential within us all.

The End.